Utopian Colleges

To The Union Institute &
University Library
at Vermont College,

Here is the story!

Constance Cappel
ph. D. '91
Constance Cappel,
Montpelier, Vermont
April 12, 2003

American University Studies

Series XIV
Education

Vol. 38

PETER LANG
New York • Washington, D.C./Baltimore • Boston
Bern • Frankfurt am Main • Berlin • Vienna • Paris

Constance Cappel

Utopian Colleges

PETER LANG
New York • Washington, D.C./Baltimore • Boston
Bern • Frankfurt am Main • Berlin • Vienna • Paris

Library of Congress Cataloging-in-Publication Data

Cappel, Constance.
Utopian colleges / Constance Cappel.
p. cm. — (American university studies. Series XIV, Education; vol. 38)
Includes bibliographical references and index.
1. Universities and colleges—United States—Sociological aspects—Case studies.
2. Education, Higher—Social aspects—United States—Case studies.
3. Education, Higher—United States—History. 4. Education, Higher—United
States—Philosophy. I. Title. II. Series.
LB2328.2.C365   378.73—dc21   98-8577
ISBN 0-8204-2056-5
ISSN 0740-4565

Die Deutsche Bibliothek-CIP-Einheitsaufnahme

Cappel, Constance:
Utopian colleges / Constance Cappel.
–New York; Washington, D.C./Baltimore; Boston; Bern;
Frankfurt am Main; Berlin; Vienna; Paris: Lang.
(American university studies: Ser. 14, Education; Vol. 38)
ISBN 0-8204-2056-5

The paper in this book meets the guidelines for permanence and durability
of the Committee on Production Guidelines for Book Longevity
of the Council of Library Resources.

For my sons, Ramsey and Anson Montgomery,
and all the people who can benefit from a
"utopian education."

Contents

Foreword

During the years 1988 to 1991, I traveled around the United States visiting over fifty institutions of higher education. They ranged from the traditional universities such as Harvard and Stanford where I spent extended periods of time with students and faculty plus observing the habits of the faculty and administrators in their private clubs and hidden offices. In contrast, I often ate at the student communal dining rooms at Sarah Lawrence, Goddard, and World College West where faculty, trustees, administrators, and students could be seen talking and eating together. These trips, conversations, and observations formed a point of view and background which lead to the researching and writing of *Utopian Colleges*. Since the first draft of this book was completed, World College West went out of business, and Caroline Shrodes Ph.D. and Harold Taylor, Ph.D. have passed away.

In 1988 I made a round-the-world trip looking for utopian colonies or similar environments. The closest to a "Heaven on Earth" that I observed was the Radha Soami Colony in Beas, the Punjab, in northern India. During the spring of 1990 I lived there for six weeks partaking of daily life and thinking about utopian colonies. Just as Sarah Lawrence College was my theoretical jumping off place in my real life search for utopian colleges and an ideal education, the Radha Soami Colony in India and its spiritual lifestyle was the starting place for my subsequent thoughts about utopian writing, American utopian colonies, and utopian colonies in general. I later returned to the colony in India many times later to verify my findings. Although I do not mention these experiences in this book, they deeply influenced the work.

Separately, and sometimes on my trips to colleges around the United States, I visited historical utopian colonies. From Fruitlands in Harvard, Massachusetts to the Amana Colonies in Iowa, most of these sites are now just museums of former utopian colonies. The few working communes I visited in California were more like patriarchal extended families than my concept of utopian colonies, but maybe that is what the 19th century American utopian colonies actually were in their time. From my visits to these many different institutions and through my conversations, interviews, readings, and research, I was able to piece together *Utopian Colleges.*

I would like to thank the people who gave of their time and thoughts which prepared the way for this book. First there was Caroline Shrodes, Ph.D. who passed away in 1991 while I was still working on the research and writing of this project. Her lively mind and support for new educational ideas was inspiring. Harold Taylor, Ph.D., who was president of Sarah Lawrence in the fifties when I was an undergraduate there, was helpful through long discussions, letters, and meetings. His historical perspective of progressive education from his friendship with John Dewey to the present climate of alternative institutions added a unique dimension to his input and critiques. He died in 1992 and is missed by his former students and friends. Robert McAndrews, Ph.D., added an international/intercultural point of view, as did Barbara Carter, Ph.D., and Michael Stone, Ed.D. Dr. McAndrews offered ideas as both a philosopher and sociologist. Michael Stone, Ed.D. as a "philosopher college president," allowed me work as an intern in the president's office while he was acting president of World College West. Barbara Carter, Ph.D., gave me a feminist and psychological perspective to my work.

Others who contributed to the research and writing of this book are Elizabeth Minnich, Ph.D., and Ed Grumbine, Ph.D. Elizabeth Minnich, the author of *Transforming Knowledge,* gave the book a critical and socially conscious reading with important suggestions. Ed Grumbine kept me on track from an environmental and holistic point of view. Others who read and responded to the work-in-progress were Judith Spock, Trustee of Antioch University; Harold and Desire Reynolds; Mary Field Belenky, author of *Women's Ways of Knowing;* and Michael Melnick, who helped with the Stanford and Harvard University background research. But most important of all was the support and love provided by my two sons, Ramsey and Anson Montgomery; and my brother, Scott H. Cappel.

For the many students, friends, college administrators, and others who helped me in my travels and research, I am grateful. I thank Jesse Tomlison of Bodega Bay, California, who translated my hand-written manuscript into a presentable typed copy. Also Christina Cappel, my niece who designed the cover and assisted in preparing the completed manuscript for publication, was an invaluable help. Mary Stephen provided a shelter at her lovely house in Stockbridge, Massachusetts where I did the final editing on this book.

Constance Cappel, Ph.D.
Radha Soami Satsang Beas
P.O. Dera Baba Saimal Singh 143204
District Amritsar
Punjab, India
March-April, 1998

Chapter 1

Introduction

What this book attempts to show is how some educational institutions broke with the dominant culture in America to create and maintain endangered enclaves which can be characterized as "utopian colleges." These places of learning all have some general characteristics in common which are not merely theoretical but are manifested in the learning and life of the institution. The hypothesis for this book is that a forward-thinking education on the college, university, and graduate level can be obtained through a student-centered, non-graded supportive educational system which has a low-faculty student ratio and has a one-to-one interchange between faculty and student. The five utopian colleges selected provided such a framework and direction.

Higher education in the 1980's went through a bleak period of anti-intellectual leadership in Washington and an undermining of budgets for an experimental curriculum. Most federal money went into science with the emphasis on the "bio" sciences which were supposedly big money makers. The military-industrial complex of the fifties and sixties seemed to have succeeded in controlling the large, prestigious, research universities. They sold their souls to big business. I tend to agree with Dr. Jackson Kytle, Goddard's former president when he writes: "With few exceptions, American institutions are drifting. Not just in the Congress or the White House; institutions, large and small, beg for leadership, for a fresh vision."[1]

The "top-down" structures of the research universities leave little interaction between the students and professors. As has been detailed in several books including Page Smith's, *Killing the Spirit: Higher Education in America*, graduate students teach and supervise the students while the professors perform in large lectures and do their own research. The five experimental colleges under study encourage close personal relationships between professors and students in their small seminar-style classes and other one-to-one situations.

All of the utopian colleges which were selected have the following characteristics in common. These utopian colleges usually have no grades; work is evaluated in written reports. Classes are small and conducted in a seminar style. The students, faculty, and administrators strive to be open-minded, while the colleges have a history of being non-sexist and non-racist. The idea of community is fostered, and the organizational structure emphasizes equality and sharing in a non-hierarchical model. The entire institutional body tends to be more idealistic than in traditional schools. Personal growth is encouraged in an interdisciplinary educational setting not based on competition but on individual accomplishment.

The five colleges which were chosen are all places with which the author was familiar either as a student, faculty member, or a nearby resident. One is located in New England, one near New York City, two in Ohio, and one on the West Coast. They were all in different stages of growth, but are all in different degrees "utopian." The institutions studied were Antioch, Goddard, Sarah Lawrence, The Union Institute, and World College West. Other institutions such as Bard, Bennington, Evergreen, Reed, Prescott, Marlboro, Friends' World College, Hampshire, The New School of Social Research, Simon's Rock of Bard College, Vermont College of Norwich University, and others could fit into the category of utopian colleges. The five colleges selected had interesting and sometimes similar histories. They all attempted to create and nurture a more humane and peace loving type of education in a cruel and warmaking world. These pockets of experimental education should be viewed as struggling examples of how a truly liberal education can be maintained in America today.

Although the information about these colleges was obtained from sources that would tend to present the colleges in their best light, a great deal of research time and a detailed investigation was devoted to each institution A written questionnaire, which was sent to a broad spectrum of individuals connected with the colleges, did not produce enough data for use in this study. Therefore, books, catalogs, historical documents, and interviews with top administrators were used to tell the story of these colleges. Their story was often presented in its most ideal light, since the institutions are reflected in the words of those who are in a public role and speak as teachers, philosophers, and advocates. The ideals of the philosopher-educators do not always translate into the realities of the colleges themselves. The colleges often flounder on the same shoals of idealistic rhetoric that caused trouble with the nineteenth century utopian communities. Survival and material needs often cause the chipping away of the high ideals, so that when the college leaders turn their backs on the utopian dream, they often make the institution more traditional and utilitarian.

These utopian colleges have also been called experimental, innovative, alternative, or progressive. Since these terms have all been used in different ways and have taken on a political nature especially in the case of "progressive," I felt that a new definition was needed for the type of education manifested in the chosen colleges. The word "utopian" came to mind, as I stood on Ralph Waldo Emerson's front lawn in Concord, Massachusetts. I had been walking at dawn mulling over the possible connections between the five colleges when I paused at Emerson's house and remembered his association with Brook Farm which is well known as a nineteenth century utopian experiment. After asking several educators what colleges came to mind when I said, "utopian colleges," I was pleased to find that they named most of the colleges that I had chosen plus others which were experimental. We all search for a utopia, a better place, and this is true also in education. In my opinion these colleges are all utopian experiments.

This insight lead to a study of utopias both real and imaginary. Both published utopias and utopian communities were examined. When theoretical utopias were studied, I found that most were written and presented in the Western male tradition and were based upon hierarchical structures. My study of American utopian communities also often revealed similar patriarchal living patterns. My concept of a utopian college was not a hierarchical or patriarchal manifestation, but one that went beyond these traditional systems to a more "ideal" form.

Both published utopias and utopian communities/communes were examined. The difficulty of living the utopian dream in communities in this world is briefly projected in this book against the generational patterns and the cultural trends in the United States in the last one hundred and fifty years. When theory becomes practice the result often takes on a different dynamic than in the original plan. The so-called realities of life or influences from the outside culture often change the course of the community. In investigating these utopian ideas translated into utopian communities an influence of the culture of the times often emerges.

Education is often a product of our culture which reflects and sometimes produces examples of current thought, and some were manifested which are the results of utopian thinking. Utopian colleges were often begun and flourished during the times of utopian thinking in the general culture. Later on in this book the history and the roots of the word "utopia" will be analyzed. The utopian colleges often had ideals that were different than the theoretical and community utopias studied. When the history of utopian literature in Western thought is examined, it contains many of the ideas of the prevailing culture. The utopian communities and communes in America often fell back into the concepts of the dominant culture after idealist beginnings.

A further hypothesis was that the individualized and small group learning which is practiced at the utopian colleges in my study is a "female" model of education as is defined in *Women's Ways of Knowing* in contrast to the patriarchal system in the research universities and which is practiced in most of higher education. In my opinion Allan Bloom and many of the conservative writers of the eighties were part of the backlash against the surge of feminism in the seventies and progressive education in general. Meanwhile, the "bio" sciences are perceived to be male and superior. I agree with Elizabeth Minnich who wrote: "Masculine 'hard' science reigns supreme over a hierarchy that slides downward to the 'soft' knowing of non quantifiable fields, approaching near bottom with the 'intuition' of women and the 'instincts' of 'primitive' people."[2] The scientific process is supposed to be fail-safe with its built in tests, but it often is as fragile to the vagaries of human error as anything in the humanities. The Challenger disaster showed the human failing of the scientific framework.

In a Carnegie report, students were accused of being without ethics and community.[3] The report said that campuses contain sexist and racist thought and actions. Although this type of thought can be attributed to being a reflection of the larger society, I think that part of the educational direction of the eighties was to destroy the liberal political gains of the sixties and seventies.

When I examined the histories of the selected colleges, I found that they went through parallel cycles with each other and of generational patterns, cycles of cultural upheavals, and feminist activity. For example, the utopian colleges originated or expanded during the same times that feminists were active: The 1850–60's (Antioch and Goddard), the 1920's (Sarah Lawrence founded and Antioch reinvented), and the 1960–70's (The Union Institute and World College West begun). Since I think that these colleges have many traits associated with the female in our psyche, they seemed to thrive when feminists were active and be under attack when misogynist thinking was in vogue. In my study of the colleges they seemed to be more successful when they functioned on a feminist model of community and sharing and became dysfunctional when they assumed a hierarchical model.

In this book I tried to examine the generational patterns, patriarchal aspects, and egalitarian styles of the published utopias, utopian communities, and utopian colleges. Selected published utopias from Plato's *Republic* to Hutchin's *University of Utopia* were examined, as were selected American utopian communities. These theoretical utopias and utopian communities were compared and contrasted to the five utopian colleges.

This book does not take the traditional approach with a theory and a practice, but instead prepares a way of thinking. In this work the author gathers and surveys the separate fields of study, so that the ground is prepared for future inquiry into the subject of "utopian colleges."

Notes

1   Kytle, Jackson. *"The President's Report." Clockworks.* Spring, 1991. p. 3.

2   Minnich, Elizabeth Kamarck. *Transforming Knowledge.* Temple University Press: Philadelphia, 1990. p. 159.

3   Wilson, Robin. "Quality of Life Said to Have Diminished on U.S. Campuses: A survey of Presidents finds Concerns over lack of 'Community.'" The Chronicle of Higher Education, Volume XXXVI, No. 33, May 3, 1990.

Chapter 2

Studies in Utopia

To understand what is "utopian" about utopian colleges, one must first look at the definition of the word "utopian," and its history in Western culture. Utopia can mean many different things to different people, cultures, and historical eras.

The word "utopia" has a common use in everyday thought and conversation, as do the phrases "Freudian slip" or "Platonic relationship." The often-used definition of "utopia" denotes an ideal; a place that is often rural and contains a community with different lifestyles and aspirations than the usual hand-to-mouth, business-oriented world of everyday. In this utopian place people are equal, caring, and good, or at least, strive to be. The dictionary definition leads in several different directions of thinking.

The Webster's Third International Dictionary defines "utopia" as:

> [fr *Utopia* an imaginary country with ideal laws and social conditions (fr Gk ou not, no + topos place) described in the book *Utopia* (1516) by Sir Thomas More + 1535 English statesman and author 1: a place (as a region, island, country, or locality) that is imaginary and indefinitely remote 2: often cap: a place, state, or condition of ideal perfection, esp. in laws, government, and social conditions (That workers ~ in which there are more jobs than men seeking them—S.E. Harris)—often used without article (many were persuaded that independence would usher in ~ A. E. Stevenson b. 1900) 3: an impractical and esp. impossibly ideal scheme, esp. for social improvement 4: a romance or other work describing a utopia (a ~ written for girls—Emory Holloway)

The dictionary definition is helpful as a starting-off place for an exploration of utopias and utopian colleges. The second definition comes the closest to the type of college analyzed in this study, even though we all know that nothing can be truly "ideal perfection." Utopias were written about by Plato, thousands of years before Sir Thomas More, and were actualized in many communities that were an important aspect of American life especially in the nineteenth century. The symbiosis between utopian thinking and American educational experiments is interwoven throughout the twentieth century. Utopian seeds grew into educational realities which were in a definite time and place.

To understand how utopian thinking applies to the colleges under consideration, a brief history of utopias must first be discussed. In Plato's *The Republic* the utopian model is of the state. Plato/Socrates outlines the ideal society within the framework of the city-state. The ideal society of a "no where" is grounded in the reality of an actual city-state, and Plato had Socrates apply his dialectical method to formulate the structure of a best possible society in which all institutions worked together to promote justice and harmony. The dialectical method allows the reader to have an imaginative creation of the city-state, in which their own utopian visions can be based. Plato's state tries to realize the divine idea of justice in this world. The ideal harmony is above this world, but it relates to this world.

Socrates built his imaginary city-state out of real needs: people come together to live a better life and exchange food, shelter, and clothing which leads to a division of labor, and each is trained for their own skill. The state grows and needs more services until the original healthy state is not self-sufficient. Soldiers are then needed. The philosopher-rulers are the heads of state and can be either male or female. Their training is again for the soul and body, and they are under constant supervision. Ownership of property is forbidden, because Socrates feels this is what makes tyrants of rulers.

Socrates felt that good education and the choice of the right leaders leads to good government, and good government leads to good education. A sense of order is established in education which determines a person's future life. He believes in positive role models and attacks bestiality when portrayed in literature, for instance when Homer describes the scene when the Trojans are slaughtered at the funeral pyre of Patroclus.

Socrates was more open to women than some of the later utopian thinkers and felt that women can share education according to their own nature. Unfortunately, he also thought that women belonged to all men in common which is an idea that future leaders of utopian communities sometimes put into practice. Plato/Socrates is hierarchical, yet the method is "standpoint."

All of these ideas and concepts contained in the ideal state of Socrates are supposed to produce happiness as shown:

> Our guardians may very likely be the happiest of men; but that our aim in founding the State was not the disproportionate happiness of any one class, but the greatest happiness of the whole; we thought that in a State which is ordered with a view to the good of the whole we should be most likely to find justice, and in the ill-ordered State injustice: and, having found them, we might then decide which of the two is the happier.[1]

The idea of happiness for the whole vs. the happiness of the individuals who make up the whole is an idea worth pondering and arises in utopian communities and colleges. How can individuals function in a community, if the community itself is not functioning? Plato/Socrates put the emphasis on the good of the whole making the needs of the individual secondary. Aristotle later criticized *The Republic*, because it emphasized an organism of total unity. The detailed regulation of the relations between the guardian class and the rest of society was designed to promote the perfect total harmony or order. Aristotle felt that this unity is bad, because it becomes perfect and is therefore impossible, because it is perfect. He felt that there must be some unity in a state, as in a household, but not an absolute total unity.

The Republic is the model upon which all other utopias are based, therefore, its features must be further defined. First, it is a small city-state where society is divided into three stratas. The ruling group is the philosophers, who have arrived at their position by a long education leading to the direct perception of the metaphysical Good. Their virtue is wisdom. The second group is the guardians, soldiers and public officials, who have been educated to practice their virtue, courage, but have not reached the stage of wisdom. The third group, which is the mass of people, are the workers (artisans and tradesmen). Their virtue is temperance which means self-restraint and obedience. A human stud farm using eugenic controls is substituted for marriage and the family for the guardian class.

Platonic thought is one of the cornerstones of Western thought and as such is now being questioned on many American college campuses by feminists and ethnic groups representing non-Western cultures, precisely because it is a basis for Western thought. In *The Republic* the idealized state grew from the culture of the time with all of its strengths and limitations. In this book the emphasis will be on educational models and will not try to analyze the entire model of the state. But the dominant culture of the time affects the writing of the theoretical utopias, so that each published utopia influences the view of education within it.

In a totalitarian and structured utopia the educational model usually will have the same emphasis. The utopia which has an army and practices eugenics probably would not be sympathetic to a self-directed and autonomous model of education. Therefore, the Platonic model of education for the upper classes which enables them to rule is what has been passed down through two thousand years of Western thought. My definition of an educational utopia is different than the Platonic model because it contains more egalitarian aspects. But one person's utopia is another person's dystopia. "Ideal perfection" for one is not for another, therefore I hope to create a definition for a "utopian college" based on the general perception of a progressive or experimental college.

The colleges studied did have some characteristics in common with Plato's utopia, but other issues such as ownership of property and producing the next generation were not applicable. Some of the colleges had philosopher kings, i.e. philosopher college presidents. They and the college community had the difficulties that Socrates/Plato touched upon with the idea that the ideal harmony is above this world, but relates to this world. The difficulties arose both in the utopian communities and colleges when concepts or ideals were made to relate to this world. Putting ideals or utopian thought into earthbound situations caused many interesting, but difficult, situations.

For over one thousand years after Socrates/Plato, the dream of utopia was not prominent. Monasteries, as the medieval universities, formed working communities which contained the educational structure that continues in our large contemporary universities. During the Middle Ages the ultimate utopia was thought to be heaven rather than a plan for better living on earth.

Thomas More in 1515–1516 wrote his book, *Utopia*, which gave us the name "utopia." This lawyer, businessman, and statesman created a world in which he attacks the values of the aristocratic classes of his day and the ethics of his fellow lawyers and businessmen. But this was an unusual lawyer/businessman who was part of a group of Christian humanists who were committed to a revival of Christian spirituality, morality, and its effectiveness in society. He had lived with the monks of Charterhouse for four years and while there he wore a hair shirt and practiced self-flagellation.[5] More came from a sixteenth century Western cultural background when he wrote *Utopia*. He borrowed from the notes of the early explorers of the New World to construct an unreal, but possibly real, island/place on earth. When he wrote his version of a better world he gathered material from the then existing world.

More's *Utopia* was an island two hundred miles long with fifty-four large, well-planned cities which were no more than a day's walk from each other. People only worked six hours a day with everyone taking a turn at farm work. The political system was a benevolent monarchy with some rudimentary checks and balances with people having more of a chance of control on the lower levels of government. More has a similar attitude as Plato in terms of property. He communizes it in order to eliminate the inequality between the rich and poor. Money is abolished, and people dress in standardized clothing. A free choice of occupation includes upward mobility. Like Plato, More places a strong emphasis on education. In *Utopia* it is a life-long process which includes erudite conversation and lectures at communal meals along with formal instruction. The purposes of education are moral and practical.

While Socrates/Plato's ideal state is supposed to reform Athens, More wrote his *Utopia* as a guide to the improvement of sixteenth century England. He thought that crime, poverty, unfair punishments, and class distinctions could be eliminated by a just and happy social order. Both men wrote from their time and culture and reflect them in their writings. One of the largest differences More had with Plato/Socrates is over the family. Usually Christian utopian writers and communities support the family as we know it in Western culture. More had wives obey their husbands, children their parents, and the younger children the older ones. This patriarchal and hierarchical arrangement is reflective of the English system of More's day and, is unfortunately, often of our present one, as well.

The problem of religion is treated in *Utopia* much the way that many colleges today treat it: an ecumenical service is available to all with the availability of all to hold private beliefs and practices. Atheists are permitted to be a part of the society, but cannot serve in the administration of Utopia. Again as a reflection of his culture, More, was far less concerned with war, than was Plato/Socrates. The inhabitants of Utopia use any excuse to keep from going to war, but if they become involved in it, they send in foreign mercenaries. More's *Utopia* was a gentler and less structured place than Plato's. In an essentially classless and democratic society, the absence of soldiers and an army make it more humane and less warlike. His family model, unfortunately, is patriarchal.

The following insight on the word "Utopia" is interesting:

> But More's book title is a pun on the Greek "ou topia" (no place) and "eu topia" (good place) and because the book is called *Utopia* or "No Place," it might be conjectured that only in Heaven (the "good place") could individuals be expected to apply so enthusiastically and disinterestedly the fundamentals of communism.[3]

Here again we have the division between heaven and earth. Because humans have not experienced "heaven," we tend to look for a "heaven on earth" or a "utopia." Since More wrote his book called *Utopia*, therefore strictly speaking whatever he puts into his society is by definition "utopian." In fact, since he coined the word, his proposed society is the most utopian of any. But utopian means different things to different people, so that an exploration of utopias and utopian communities with their many different views and outcomes is necessary to achieve the historical background in order to look at "utopian colleges."

Utopian writing continued through the publication a century later of Johann Valentin Andreae's *Christianopolis* (1619) which depicts an ideal Christian city. In 1627 Sir Francis Bacon's *The New Atlantis* presents a world that is a composite of Plato and More. But his Atlantis does not believe in Spartan garb and its inhabitants are attired in extravagantly sumptuous dress and jewels, which is different than most functionally dressed inhabitants of fictional and communal utopias. Another interesting new aspect of Bacon's work is his creation of a research institute which is a prototype of the large educational research institutions of our times.

At about the same time that Bacon wrote *The New Atlantis*, Thomas Campanella wrote *The City of The Sun*. A Dominican friar, Campanella was constantly persecuted for his ideas. He was questioned by the Spanish Inquisition seven times and spent twenty-seven years in jail. He finally came under the protection of Richelieu, who helped him receive a royal pension, so that he was able to live peacefully until the age of seventy-one in the Convent of the Dominicans. He did not have to die for his views, as did More and Socrates, but was victimized by his culture and wished for a better world.

The City of The Sun makes clear that Campanella's background was as a monk. The ideas of Christianity are woven throughout the work. The people live in dormitories with public dining halls, which were similar to the living arrangements in the monastic way of life. His utopia again emphasizes eugenics, education, and the aristocracy of merit and education. His seven-walled city is a veritable classroom and museum with permanent exhibits of all kinds, because Campanella felt that students learned better from real things rather than from pictures and models. This idea is similar to some of the tenets found in progressive education.

Utopian writing did not flourish in the eighteenth century, but in the nineteenth century both the real and imaginary utopias shifted from Europe to the United States. Of the nineteenth century theoretical utopias, the most important is Edward Bellamy's *Looking Backward* (1888). Bellamy was an avid reader and a student of political economy, history, and religion. He was acquainted with both the American and European radical thinkers of his time. In Bellamy's book reviews and editorials in his family-owned *Springfield Union* in the 1879's, he mentioned Robert Owen, John Noyes, Bronson Alcott, Emerson, and Thoreau and others associated with the Owenite, Fourieristic, and Transcendentalist movements.[4]

During the nineteenth century many religious or socialist colonies were flourishing, which were referred to at the time as utopian. Bellamy was familiar with these, as well as with the utopian literature of his day. Bellamy, after reading Hawthorne's *Blithedale Romance* , agreed with him that a colony was not the test of the workability of the doctrines that it supported. Bellamy felt that only a completely new state could test the practical aspects of any plan, therefore he thought that a single step taken toward reform in society made a more permanent gain than the most successful colony. Bellamy stated: "We do not believe in the colony idea as a help to the social solution any more than we believe in the monastic idea as an assistance to the moral solution. We cannot help thinking they would serve their generation better by staying at home and preaching the gospel to their neighbors."[5]

Looking Backward, Bellamy's most famous book, is about Julian West, an upper-class Bostonian who goes into a state of suspended animation in 1887 and awakes in 2000. From a mean and unjust Boston in 1887, West awakes to one where the nation has taken over the means of production and created humans who act out of altruistic impulses, because of the new environment. Bellamy's world is a socialistic state with a civilian army doing the work. Money has been abolished, and the state, as we know it, has withered away. Since economic competition has been abandoned, wars are no longer necessary. Everything is socialist except his family system which is Victorian. Women are supposedly equal, although his writing about his romance with a descendent of his old fiancée is syrupy, maudlin, and paternalistic.

But Bellamy's view of higher education was prophetic and reflects his familiarity with Horace Mann's work. He wrote:

> Dr. Leete answered "It was not college education but college dissipation and extravagance which cost so highly [referring to 1887]. The actual expense of your college appears to be very low, and would have been far lower if their patronage had been greater. The higher education nowadays is as cheap as the lower, as all grades of teachers, like all other workers, receive the same support. We have simply added to the common school system of compulsory education, in vogue in Massachusetts a hundred years ago, a half dozen grades, carrying the youth to the age of twenty-one and giving him what you used to call the education of a gentleman, instead of turning him loose at fourteen or fifteen with no mental equipment beyond reading, writing and the multiplication tables."[6]

By 1887 Horace Mann had already been the first president of Antioch College and had brought a more liberated version of a non-sexist and non-racist higher education to realization than the public education/economic model which Bellamy envisioned.

A later president of Antioch was fascinated by Edward Bellamy and even wrote two books about him. Arthur Morgan, the "pragmatic utopian" president of Antioch in the 1920's thought that "it was the genius of Edward Bellamy that he took Utopia out of the region of hazy dreamland and made it a concrete program for the actual modern world."[7]

Morgan in his defense of Bellamy makes the following strong statement about Bellamy and utopian thinking in general.

> Bellamy was a utopian. He looked upon the tragedies of human affairs as mostly due to causes under human control, and not irremovably innate in nature. As to the physical work, he risked making a fool of himself by carelessly assuming many inventions which were necessary to his purpose. He almost implied that in the physical world the limits of man's desire set the only limits to what he might create. At a time when "sensible" men protected themselves against the charge of being utopian by refraining from such wild suggestions, Bellamy assumed the existence of television, broadcasting, air

travel, air conditioning, automobiles, mechanical calculators, concrete high-
ways, farm tractors, and the controlled acceleration of plant growth.[8]

As a visionary writer Bellamy forecast in *Looking Backward* the
future utopia in Boston in 2000. Since we are near to that date, it is
interesting to see how close to reality he was, just as it is interesting to
see whether the year 1984 had any relation to George Orwell's book
of the same name. The industrial army and the lack of crime are not
translated from Bellamy's utopian Boston to the present day one, although he did try to imagine our world as a more humane place than
it is. But he was sure of one thing that would be as true in 2000 as in
1887: the Boston shoreline. But he was wrong, since the edge of the
harbor has been moved by human ingenuity. But crime and unfair
distribution of wealth are still major problems, as they were in 1887.

Edward Bellamy's work continued utopian thinking into the twentieth century, but his concept of a superstate which would regulate life
down to its minute details soon lost its appeal. Both totalitarianism
and industrial capitalism produced examples in the twentieth century
of the misuse of science and technology against people, turning individuals' lives into nightmares, not dreams. The utopian type of literature since World War II reflects the disillusionment of what might have
been previously utopian writing, but instead became dystopias and
anti-utopian works.

The intentional dystopias of Aldous Huxley's *Brave New World*
(1932) and *Brave New World Revisited* (1958) present the world
controlled by technology. The eugenics of previous utopians are replaced by a medical manipulation made possible through the science
of genetics. In many ways we are living in a *Brave New World,* and
we have also passed the date of George Orwell's *1984* . One of the
few contemporary writers of modern utopias was B. F. Skinner in his
books, *Walden Two* and *Beyond Freedom and Dignity.*

Fontaine Maury Belford, former dean at The Union Institute, wrote
in 1980:

> And this is why in the study of utopias we must engage ourselves not only in
> the history we know, but in the history that is to come. To design a utopia is
> to engage in an act of vision. It entails pressing beyond the constraints of the
> crises in which we live and moving into a new order of possibility. Visionary
> activity is not an *extra* in society any longer, as if it ever was. It is the only
> thing that has any chance of carrying us from the world in which we presently
> live—which is destroying itself at such a rate that life within it cannot long be

a possibility—to a world that is informed by new values and a new understanding of being. For this transformation cannot take place in think tanks
and high-powered conferences. It will be brought about by a revolution in our
imagination's exercise; by the dreaming up of new utopias. Plato, Thomas
More, Bronson Alcott projected the perfection of human personality. We,
more modestly, cherish the hope of survival.[9]

Educators and students, administrators and trustees, faculty and
concerned citizens, all must think in a utopian, not dystopian, way
about higher education today. While our country and the world continue in their destructive course, we must have the courage to plan
and dream for a better future, even if it never comes into fruition. We
must not lose the ability to dream and make the plans for our dreams.

But one educator did just this, and he wrote a book about a utopian
higher educational institution in a contemporary setting. In 1953
Robert M. Hutchins presented a series of lectures at the University of
Chicago which were later published as *The University of Utopia*. His
fictional utopia is located in the Western world in a place that has the
climate, but nothing else, of southern California. He further defines it:

It is a scientific, industrial democracy. It is rich and powerful. It is surrounded
by enemy states. It is committed to the doctrine of education for all. Its principal educational problem has been to determine how to educate everybody,
so that the country may have the scientific and industrial strength it requires
and at the same time educate everybody so that the country will know how to
use its scientific and industrial power wisely. I hope that the masterly solution
of this problem at which the Utopians have arrived may commend itself to
you. At the end I shall inquire whether it is possible for the United States
which has the same problem, to adopt the same solution.[10]

Hutchins is taking the classic historical utopian point of view towards the problem. He has created a separate country, similar to the
one which he hopes to criticize, and has given it a "Utopian" society
which is different. In this context he places his "utopian university."
He feels that first the society must be different, in order that the university be better.

In my study of utopian colleges, they are analyzed as existing in our
contemporary society and not in a fictional one. They exist as examples or experiments much as the utopian communities did, and as
such have many disagreements and differences of opinion with the
prevalent American culture. Hutchins, on the other hand, removes his
university to a fictional society where he can better illustrate his points.

His premise is different than mine in that he sees his university educating all for scientific and industrial "strength" and "power" for use in a society with the same values. His university laboratory is for producing educated citizens for the society rather than producing humane and original thinkers which might run counter to "scientific" and "industrial" constraints.

Hutchins deals with the problems of vocational training and the use of the worker's free time. He bemoans vocational training in universities and attacks the American public as desiring money, power, and publicity. He feels it is impossible that "an educational system dedicated to industrial power can produce the wisdom that a country needs to use its power in its own best interests, to say nothing of those of the human race."[11]

Hutchins creates the people of his utopia to encourage science, but not industrial strength, military power, or more gadgets. The utopians in his society reserve highest honors for distinguished thinkers and artists. He feels that the arts in America in 1953 "have become a mere decoration, or a recreation for females not gainfully employed."[12] At this point Hutchins reflects the culture of his time in the American 1950's, but it makes one pause and wonder whether a "female not gainfully employed" would ever be eligible to be classified as receiving "highest honors" as a "distinguished artist" no matter what talent she exhibited.

In his book, Hutchins does attack specialization in a scientific institution. He believes in an interdisciplinary approach when he comments that: "I take it that the aim of education is not to gain more and more detailed knowledge of the world but to understand the world and ourselves in it."[13] He believes that a professor of American history should be able to teach English history in a liberal arts college instead of being "an uneducated holder of a Ph.D."[14]

Hutchin's University of Utopia is divided into institutions with faculties numbering about twenty-five and a student body of about two hundred and fifty. Each faculty and student group contains representatives of the major fields, so that they will all have contact with each other's area of learning. The College of Utopia begins in the junior year in high school and ends with the sophomore year of the conventional American college much like the British system. As Hutchins writes: "The object of the College of Utopia is to see to it that everybody in it gets a liberal education. One object of the University of Utopia is to see to it that he does not lose it when he has got it."[15]

These ideas of Hutchins are interesting observations, since many utopian colleges and communities had a vibrant life when they were under two hundred and fifty participants, but formed competing factions when they grew larger. Also the idea of the last two years of high school combined with the first two years of college to give the "college experience" is not new and was temporarily used at Goddard. What the five utopian colleges did was make the entire four undergraduate years the mixture of what Hutchins divides into "college" and "university" experience. He seems to envision a community college leading into a university experience rather than four years of liberal arts leading to a B.A. and then progressing to graduate school.

Hutchin's University of Utopia has philosophical diversity where all members of the community can think and communicate with one another. He believes in a philosophy of education and is against a custodial system. Hutchins writes that: "The Utopians think that intellectual development is too important to be left to amateurs; and, since they are devoted to democracy, they do not see how they can maintain and improve their democracy unless every citizen has the chance to become as wise as he can."[16]

The University of Utopia has many of the other qualities of the utopian colleges, in that almost all the teaching is conducted through discussion, and the credit system was never introduced. Centers of residential adult education in his Utopia are available, such as at Sarah Lawrence and were at World College West, and are integral in the adult education programs of Goddard, Antioch, and Union. Learning takes the place of vacation as we know it. The qualifications of the professors at the University of Utopia are that they must be eminent in their field, as in traditional American universities, but they must also be willing and able to receive and shed light in other fields. This interdisciplinary approach is similar to the one emphasized in The Union Institute and other utopian colleges studied.

The University of Utopia was conceived and established as a center of independent thought with extra curricular activities but no football team. Again Hutchins reflects another of the characteristics of the utopian colleges studied which are all centers of independent thought without having the strong athletic programs of traditional universities. Hutchins feels that: "The object of the University of Utopia is not to mirror the chaos of the world but to straighten it out."[17]

Robert Hutchins in his chapter, "Social and Political Conformity," looks at the differences between European universities which he thinks are based on "a corporation of students wanting to learn or teachers wanting to teach,"[18] against the American university which "was a corporation formed by a religious denomination or the state."[19] None of the colleges under consideration are denominational or formed by the state, but instead work in an environment where students/learners wish to learn and faculty teach.

Hutchins sums up the problem of American higher education when he writes:

> This attitude helps to transform an educational system into a custodial sys-
> tem, and a custodial system tends to confirm this attitude. If one object of a
> university or of an educational system is to indoctrinate the young with the
> common opinion, the doctrine of adjustment to the environment becomes
> one thing the community most immediately needs is citizens who have been
> indoctrinated with the common opinion. Thus we come to view a university
> as a place in which the young are familiarized with the tribal mores and in
> which other activities immediately useful to the community are carried on.[20]

Unfortunately, Robert Hutchins locates his University of Utopia in the country of fictional Utopia when he makes the following statement: "The reason why the University of Utopia is so utopian is that the people of Utopia are utopians."[21] To have his University of Utopia reflect the thinking and direction of the American culture, the culture would have to be non-materialistic and totally different than it is.

The utopian colleges which I have studied have existed in the American culture and have often brought the best aspects of it into their midst while rejecting detrimental cultural mores. They seem to try to create a utopian culture. These colleges have thrived when the American culture was open minded and forward thinking and have become embattled when the times were close minded. The seeds of change fostered in these colleges often remain alive in the American culture but underground. Hutchin's University of Utopia must be located in Utopia in order to exist, while the five utopian colleges studied attempted to integrate many of the positive aspects of the utopian education he described on a daily basis, while existing in the very real world.

Many utopias have similar themes and lifestyles. In the Western utopian tradition from Plato to the present, I would like to illustrate some of their general qualities. Religion is not the unifying factor in the written tradition of utopia, in contrast to the many earthly communes and religious communities which attempted to construct a "heaven on earth." The moral standards of published utopias are fairly strict with most of one's attention going toward the job to be done rather than individual self-expression. The sexual drive is channeled into producing eugenic children. The authors of imaginary utopias tend to think that the happiness of the individual is produced by the perfect society and by being a good citizen. The social structure of Western utopias is usually based on the Socratic/Platonic system of three classes with the power residing in a non-hereditary aristocracy. Rarely are checks and balances used to create a working democracy.

Education is a continuous theme of utopia, ranging from being provided as a privilege of the upper classes to the more general accessibility of everyone. Education creeps into all aspects of life from the communal eating arrangements which are supposed to encourage intellectual exchanges to structured learning. Character building and physical exercise are interwoven with social adjustment. All of the parts must fit a harmonious whole society. Education as a preparation for your lifework is supposed to be pleasurable. The economic system of utopia is usually socialistic, and the younger generation does most of the dirty work. Retirement can begin at fifty. Everybody works, and conspicuous consumption no longer exists. Everyone dresses simply, lives simply, and there is enough to go around.

No firm consensus is available for family life where the writer's imagination and desires are reflected in their written work. When family men write utopias, they want happy paternalistic families. The state inherits property, not heirs. Utopia only goes as far as a human's imagination can take it. Much of what is conceived is often in reaction to the culture or the time of the writer; for instance, Socrates/Plato had a dim view of democracy while to others it is the highest form of government. Most utopian writers agree about work and society, but they often look at life in utopia as a top-down structure.

Unlike the male utopian writers, twentieth century feminists and visionaries question the basic assumption of power based on one's gender, as did Plato. In the male utopias the question of childbearing and rearing had always been conceptualized from a male point of view. For the state to continue, a new generation had to be produced. The male utopian writers often approached this problem through eugenics and other controlled experiments while some favored the paternalistic family model. The problem of perpetuating the next generation was also central in the nineteenth century communities. These communes approached the problem through different avenues from celibacy to a type of eugenics controlled and heavily utilized by a patriarch. The utopian colleges are not faced with such a dilemma. Colleges also must recruit and interest students in order to continue. The utopian colleges, on the whole, address the issues of the dominant culture and try to respond with more equal solutions than in traditional colleges. Their system of sharing and teaching often produces a more harmonious way of working rather than the authoritarian, hierarchical way used at most traditional colleges. Usually each voice can be heard in a utopian college.

Utopian writing for contemporary life is often expressed not only in dystopias but also in science fiction. Most of the feminist utopian writing has been expressed in this form, and in these writings sex roles have been eliminated. These writings are rooted in the utopian tradition and as such have similarities with the male genre of science fiction. They usually have pastoral settings, centralize the positive uses of science and technology, and use space and time travel as a narrative device. The differences in the feminist versions is that the main characters are women, and technology is secondary to the creation of a society where power is shared. They look at the world from a feminist perspective and see the need for change as do all utopian writers. Doris Lessing's *Shikasta* and *Memoirs of a Survivor* portray a future after a holocaust where psychic communication is vital. Women's psychic abilities are again emphasized in Sally Gearhart's *The Wanderground*.

Two utopian novels, *The Female Man* by Joanna Russ and *Woman on the Edge of Time* by Marge Piercy, are feminist models for an ideal world. They have many elements in common with other utopian works, such as equitable distribution of resources and authority, flexibility of work, status based on individual worth, and a pastoral setting which encourages a respect for the environment. Unlike the male utopian works, these novels criticize patriarchal power distributions and relationships where men control the resources and decision making. They do not assume that nurturing is only a female characteristic or that violence is exclusive to the male. Sophisticated technology makes childbearing not gender-controlled.

The interesting aspects for this study of utopias and utopian colleges were the use of power in these two feminist utopias. The power is not held by a strong charismatic leader, but by loose associations or a benevolent anarchy which replaces formal governmental structure. Leadership is voluntary and rotates, and individual self-development is primary. Disagreements are resolved in community meetings. Much of the learning done at utopian colleges is under the above conditions.

In summary, the previously examined studies in utopia show the changes in utopian thought from Plato\Socrates to Marge Piercy. The many attempts to dream and plan for a better world reflect each writer's gender, class, time, and bias. When the utopian writing is examined in the light of each author's point of view, the opinions create the type of utopia planned. The "good of the whole" is often a value judgment of the particular creator who wishes to create their own version of utopia. The creation of a utopia is a creation of a world with Godlike powers taken by the human creators who show their many human limitations, as has been shown in this examination of utopian writing.

Notes

1   Plato's *The Republic*. Translated by B. Jowett, M.A. Vintage Books: New York, p. 421.

2   Davis, J.C. *Utopia and the ideal society: A study of English utopia writing, 1516–1700*, Cambridge University Press: Cambridge, England, 1981. p. 45.

3   Genovese, E.N., "Paradise and the Golden Age: Ancient Origins of the Heavenly Utopia," Sullivan, E.D.S., ed. *The Utopian Vision: Seven Essays on the Quincentennial of Sir Thomas More*. San Diego State University Press, San Diego, CA, 1983.

4   Bowman, Sylvia E., et . al. *Edward Bellamy Abroad: An American Prophet's Influence*. Twayne Publishers: New York, 1962, p. 46.

5   Ibid, p. 49.

6   Bellamy, Edward, *Looking Backward,* Harper & Brothers: New York, 1959. p. 210.

7   Morgan, Arthur E. *Edward Bellamy*. Columbia University Press: New York, 1944. p. ix.

8   Ibid, p. xxi.

9   Belford, Fontaine Maury. "Yesterday's Dream, Tomorrow's Necessity," in Moment, Gairdner B. and Kraushaar, Otto F. (ed). *Utopias: the American Experience*. The Scarecrow Press, Inc.; Metuchen, N.J. 1980. p. 245.

10 Hutchins, Robert M. *The University of Utopia*. The University of Chicago Press: Chicago, 1953, p. 2.

11 Ibid, p. 13.

12 Ibid, p. 17.

13 Ibid, p. 24.

14 Ibid, p. 35.

15 Ibid, p. 45.

16 Ibid, p. 55.

17 Ibid, p. 70.

18 Ibid, p. 77.

19 Ibid, p. 77.

20 Ibid, p. 82.

21 Ibid, p. 96.

Bibliography

1. Bellamy, Edward. *Looking Backward.*. Harper & Brothers: New York, 1888, 1959.

2. Bogulaw, Robert: *The New Utopias: A Study of System Design and Social Change*. Prentice-Hall: Englewood Cliffs, NJ, 1965.

3. Bowman, Sylvia E. et al. *Edward Bellamy Abroad: An American Prophet's Influence*. Twayne Publishers: New York, 1962.

4. Campanella, Tommaso. *The City of The Sun: A Poetical Dialogue*. (1568–1639), University of California Press: Berkeley, 1981.

5. Chavannes, Albert. *The Future Commonwealth*. Arno Press & The New York Times, 1892, 1981.

6. Cornish, Edward. *The Study of the Future: An Introduction to the Art and Science of Understanding and Shaping Tomorrow's World*. World Future Society: Washington, D.C., 1983.

7. Davis, J.C. *Utopia and the ideal society: A study of English utopian writings: 1516–1700*. Cambridge University Press: Cambridge, England, 1981.

8. Dodd, Anna Bowman. *The Republic of the Future or Socialism a Reality*. Cassell & Company: New York, 1887.

9. Eramus, Charles J. *In Search of The Common Good: Utopian Experiments Past and Future*. Free Press: New York, 1977.

10. Fogarty, Robert S. *Dictionary of American Communal and Utopian History*. Greenwood Press: Westport, Conn., 1980.

11. Gearhart, Sally. *The Wanderground*. Persephone Press: Watertown, MA. 1979.

12. Geissler, Ludwig A. *Looking Beyond*. Arno Press & The New York Times: New York, (1891), 1971.

13. Hertzler, Joyce Oramel. *The History of Utopian Thought*. Macmillan: New York, 1923.

14. Huxley, Aldous. *Brave New World*. Harper & Row: New York, 1932.

15. Huxley, Aldous. *Brave New World Revisited*. Harper & Row: New York, 1965.

16. *Ideal Commonwealths: Plutarch's Lycurgus, More's Utopia, Bacon's New Atlantic, Campanella's City of the Sun*. With an introduction by Henry Morley. Routledge: London, 1885.

17. Kirby, Georgiana Bruce. *Years of Experience: An Autobiographical Narra-tive.* AMS: New York, 1971 (first published 1887).

18. Lessing, Doris. *Memoirs of a Survivor.* Knopf: New York, 1975.

19. Lessing, Doris. *Shikasta.* Knopf: New York, 1979.

20. Manuel, Frank E. and Fritzie P. *Utopian Thought in the Western World.* The Belknap Press of Harvard University Press: Cambridge, MA., 1980.

21. *Modern Man in Search of Utopia.* San Francisco Alternatives Foundation, 1971.

22. More, Sir Thomas. *Utopia.* Ed. Collins, J. Churton. Oxford University Press: London, 1961.

23. More, Sir Thomas. *Utopia.* Edited, with introduction and notes, Collins, J. Churton. Clarendon Press: Oxford, England, 1909

24. Morgan, Arthur E. *Edward Bellamy.* Columbia University Press: New York, 1944.

25. Morgan, Arthur E. *Nowhere Was Somewhere: How History Makes Utopias and Utopias Make History.* University of North Carolina Press: Chapel Hill, N.C., 1946.

26. Morgan, Arthur E. *The Philosophy of Edward Bellamy.* King's Crown Press: New York, 1945.

27. Mumford, Lewis. *The Story of Utopias.* With an introduction by Hendrik Willem Van Loon. Smith: Gloucester, Mass., 1959.

28. Orwell, George. *1984.* Harcourt, Brace: New York, 1949.

29. Nozick, Robert. *Anarchy, State, and Utopia.* New York: Basic Books, 1944.

30. Ozmon, Howard. *Utopias and Education.* Burgess Publishing Co., 1969.

31. Plato. *The Republic.* Modern Library: New York, 1982.

32. Piercy, Marge. *Woman on the Edge of Time.* Knopf: New York, 1976.

33. Plattel, Martin G. *Utopian and Critical Thinking.* Duquesne University Press: Pittsburgh, PA, 1972.

34. Russ, Joanna. *The Female Man.* Bantam: New York, 1979.

35. Skinner, B. F. *Beyond Freedom and Dignity.* Knopf: New York, 1971.

36. Skinner, B. F. *Walden Two.* Macmillan: New York, 1976.

37. *Utopian Studies 1.* Edited by Beauchamp, Gorman, Roemer, Kenneth, Smith, Nicholas D. University Press of America: New York, 1987.

38. Walsh, Chade. *From Utopia to Nightmare.* Greenwood Press, Publishers: Westport, Connecticut, 1962,

39.   Weiss, Miriam Strauss. *A Lively Corpse*. A. S. Barnes and Co.: New York, 1969.

40.   Wells, H.G. *A Modern Utopia*. Thomas Nelson & Sons: London, 1930.

41.   Wells, H.G. *The Open Conspiracy*. Doubleday: Garden City, N.Y., 1928.

Chapter 3

American Utopian Communities

The history of published utopias is even more interesting when it is examined against actual American utopian experiments which flourished in the nineteenth century. These temporal communities dealt with the daily lives of their inhabitants and gave examples of how difficult it is to turn theory into fact or to create a working utopian community on earth.

The theoretical utopias portray a better world in contrast to the realities of this one. When More named his fictional island, "Utopia" meaning "no place," he might have played with the word "eutopia" meaning "good place" which is pronounced the same way. He possibly suggested the existence of a "good place" (maybe Heaven) which was really "no place" (anywhere on earth). But again he may have meant "no place on earth at present." "Dystopia," which means "bad place," has become the word used to describe pessimistic fictional views of the future. Thomas More's utopia was of a perfect society that once formed remained the same. Published utopias give us finite positive worlds while the dystopias project a finite negative and frightening world. But what about eutopias, those good places located in our not-so-perfect world? Or the second definition of "utopia" which was "a place, state, or condition of ideal perfection?"

During the nineteenth century in the United States many communal "good places" sprang up. I will continue to use the word "utopia," since that is the common use of the word, rather than "eutopia," but I will mean often "good place" or "place or condition of ideal perfection" when referring to these communal experiments. Many of these over two hundred places lasted a short time, but some lasted over thirty-five years or into a second generation.

One of the primary and longest-lived groups is the Shakers which became a communal movement around 1800 and have continued until our era. A few Shakers still live in Canterbury, New Hampshire and Sabbathday Lake, Maine. Another group, the Rappites Zoarites had a life of about 80 years from 1819 to 1898 while the famous Oneida community had only been a commune for thirty-seven years when in 1881 it incorporated. Only the Hutterites, begun in Europe in 1528, are still strong today of all the nineteenth century American communities. Communal farming communities which last more than one generation are rare.

The nineteenth century community experiments were also called communes. In America, they had two peak periods: from 1800 to 1860 and in the late 1960's. Few were begun after the Civil War and by 1900 only a few existed. The communal movement seemed to be dead for the next sixty-five years.

The dates of the origin of the nineteenth century major communes are as follows;

Commune	Starting Date
Snowhill	1800
Harmony	1804
Zoar	1841
Brook Farm	1841
Hopedale	1841
Northampton	1842
Amana	1843
North American Phalanx	1843
Bethel	1848
Oneida	1848[2]

Many of the successful nineteenth-century communes began as Christian congregations and adopted collective consumption and production. Some of the most successful were the German separationist movements, such as the Hutterites, which faced the tribulations of frontier-settlement conditions. Several of the more prominent communities are examined with the history of their successes and failures.

As mentioned before one of the longest-lived groups were the Shakers which have existed from 1773. At their peak in 1830 they totaled some nineteen communities divided into seventy-two communes, but in 1974 only two communes with twelve elderly women survived. The Shakers addressed the difficult question of family in a unique way: celibacy. The sect was founded by Ann Lees in Manchester, England, after four of her children died in infancy. She thought that co-habitation was the source of all evil because of the death of her offspring, so that celibacy became one of the tenets of the group. They added members who already had children and adopted children from the outside world to continue their survival.

Women joined the Shakers in a ratio of two to one, and since 1961 all members of the United Society have been female. In the nineteenth century the Shaker community was a haven for widows and for women with young children, since life insurance and salaried jobs for women were almost unknown then. For many of the Believers the economic security attracted them, since "they simply had no desire to engage in the day-to-day tumult of a competitive system. Such individuals found a more relaxed atmosphere and a more secure way of life within the confines of a communistic organization."[3]

According to scholarly opinion, the social aspects of Shaker life also probably drew as many people as did the economic.[4] Group living and sharing of everyday tasks, socialization with like-minded people and emotional security, all of these elements had an appeal. Such an appeal is also often found in the utopian colleges which provide an alternative from the competitive stance of traditional universities with grading systems and commercialized sports. These colleges often provide a community of like-minded individuals.

The Shakers were a feminist type of society. Their beginnings originated from Mother Ann of whom "a fair number of Americans also concluded that Mother Ann was indeed the feminine incarnation of Christ."[5] Being a celibate order, they used conversion to increase their number. James Whittaker and Lucy Wright succeeded Mother Ann and built up the organization for ten years. In 1796, upon the death of Whittaker, Mother Lucy assumed the leadership for twenty-five years.

Throughout the Shaker communities, common ownership was practiced. They had no rich or poor, masters or slaves, no bosses or underlings. As William A. Kephart observes:

> Such a system, admittedly, constituted what sociologists call an *ideal* type; that is, a hypothetical situation where all the preconceived criteria are met or where everything goes according to plan. The ideal type has value that it enables the sociologist to compare the actual situation with the conceptualized ideal. In this sense, the Believers came reasonably close to attaining their ideal.[6]

Possibly one of the reasons that the Shaker communities had such a long and productive communal life was that they worked and lived in a non-hierarchical structure. Their communes shared among the members. But in terms of higher education, no Shaker went on to college which in my opinion was a negative aspect of Shaker life. Younger members who had an intellectual curiosity usually left by the age of twenty-one. Education consisted of the basics of English, arithmetic, and geography. Fine arts were not encouraged, but the manual arts produced handicraft products such as brooms, spinning wheels, and baskets which are prized by antique collectors today for their simple, aesthetic appeal.

The aspects of Shaker life pertinent to this study are the longevity of their communities to other utopian communities and the non-hierarchical system of living and working which makes their community life one that is similar to those of some utopian colleges. The aspect of their system of sharing and working cooperatively is also emulated in many of the utopian colleges.

Another nineteenth century community experiment was Brook Farm which was also one of the best-known. Since Brook Farm was founded by intellectuals and contained many famous writers, there are many accounts of its brief six year life. Because this community had intellectual and educational origins, it also contains many of the same dreams as the utopian colleges do.

Brook Farm was founded in the mid-nineteenth century by George Ripley, a Unitarian minister who felt after fourteen years of preaching at the Purchase Street Unitarian Church in Boston, that he was not bringing anyone closer to Christ by his oratory. He was supported in his plans for Brook Farm by the Transcendentalists, a group located in Boston that met to discuss philosophy, literature, and social problems. This erudite group included Ralph Waldo Emerson, Ripley, Ellory Channing, Elizabeth Peabody, Margaret Fuller, Henry Thoreau, Bronson Alcott, and others. They envisioned Brook Farm as devoted to agriculture and education. Ownership was to be vested in members holding one or more shares at $500.00 each. All members, men and women, were to work and receive equal pay, from which they would pay for their board with a little left over for their personal needs.

Since many of the members of Brook Farm were excellent teachers, their school was a success. They introduced the first kindergarten in the United States under the direction of Elizabeth Peabody and based their method of education on work. Every child had some definite task to perform. Since everyone in the community worked and was interested in cultural pursuits, the children learned from example. Every evening there was music, singing, dancing, and discussion.[7]

The founders of Brook Farm were more philosophers and educators than they were farmers and business people. But the community, which started without any working capital, ended the second year with a surplus of $500.00. Hard work and a shared intellectual ideal made the community financially sufficient even without a business orientation of its members.

After the expansion, or first generation phase originating from the original plan, is where many businesses, colleges, and communities run into trouble. In the case of Brook Farm, the original colonists were persuaded by Albert Brisbane and Horace Greeley to turn their community into a Fourierist Phalanx. Brook Farm was a small, working community of idealists, intellectuals, and creative people who had achieved a reasonable lifestyle. They were paying their bills, living together without much friction, sharing tasks, schooling their own and outside children, and living at peace with the surrounding communities. Because they were so successful, Greeley chose them for the Fourierist experiment, which was political and hierarchical, not intellectually based as was Brook Farm.

Albert Brisbane, a wealthy young man from Buffalo, encountered the teachings of Charles Fourier in France. Fourier had developed a detailed scheme for the entire reorganization of society. Fourier adopted Robert Owen's idea of small productive communities, but he differed in his concept of property as being more capitalistic than socialistic. He conceptualized the organization of each of the communities from work to each individual's relationship to another. The communities were called "phalanxes" and consisted of between 1,600 and 2,000 people. The phalanxes were divided into groups of three to seven people who worked in a "series" which would make up a "harmony." The pyramid effect would continue with phalanxes from over the world uniting into a central body located in Constantinople.

Charles Fourier lead a lonely, uneventful life. He never married, had no lasting amorous liaisons, spent most of his life in cheap hotels, and had disciples, but no friends. The system he evolved provides unlimited sex for everyone, communal life, good food and good company at table, plus an ideal of rural and urban housing. Did the barrenness of his life create the fantasy of his utopia? In the appendix of *Letters from Brook Farm 1841–1847,* Anna Parsons who knew Fourier as "a person of a great deal of power," thought he seemed as "one who sported with misery and brings the laugh of the insane to my mind."[8]

Emerson, as he often did with many others, summed up the Frenchman's character when he said that Fourier "had skipped no fact but one, namely, 'Life' and that he carries a whole French revolution

in his head, and much more."[9] Emerson also saw through the philosophical pretensions of Brisbane when he commented that "Brisbane
in his earnestness made everything reducible to order,—even 'the hy-
ena, the jackal, the gnat, the bug, the flea, were all beneficial parts of
the system, but it took 1680 men to make one Man.'" [10]

How did it happen that Brook Farm changed after two successful
years of institutional life from an "association of individuals" into a
Phalanx? Swift records that: "The various recollections say only in a
dim way that at about this time there was much talk of a change, and
that finally it was effected principally through the influence of
Brisbane."[11] After much debate between the communal (Fourierist) and
associative (Brook Farm) ideals, on January 18, 1844 a second edition of the constitution of the Brook Farm Association was printed in
the magazine, *Present*. This edition was prefaced by Ripley, Pratt,
and Dana, who after summarizing the existing conditions and advan-
tages of the Farm, continued: "With a view to the ultimate expansion
into a perfect Phalanx, we desire without any delay to organize the
three primary departments, namely Agriculture, Domestic Industry,
and the Mechanic Arts."[12] A decision was quickly reached after the
December convention, and Brook Farm became a Fourierist Phalanx.

When Brook Farm fell under the Fourierist direction, it admitted
many new members at one time, and most of them were artisans not
intellectuals. Brook Farm changed from a like minded group of idealists who taught and worked together harmoniously to a community
consumed with building a large, Phalanstery building and assimilating
the artisans and their families. But great names continued to be involved with Brook Farm, as Emerson described the participants when
he wrote: "In and around Brook Farm, whether as members, board-
ers, or visitors, were many remarkable persons, for character, intellect
or accomplishments."[13]

Brook Farm met its end when Albert Brisbane and Horace Greeley
took it over as one of the most successful communities of its day, in
order to make it an example of Fourierism. Many New York newspapers attacked anything connected with Fourier at that time. The neighbors and parents of Brook Farm students read these newspapers and
were suspected of burning down the almost-finished Phalanstery building. The financial loss of the burnt building and the change of ideals
caused the community to break up. According to Swift: "In two years
more the tide of Fourierism had begun to ebb, and it carried out with
it Brook Farm."[14] The North American Phalanx at Red Bank, NJ,

which lasted fourteen years, and the Ceresco Phalanx in Wisconsin soon collapsed leaving Fourierism dead in America.

Swift concludes his book about Brook Farm with the following paragraph.

> Brisbane's own career as a doctrinaire properly closed with the ominous silence of Greeley and the ineluctable misadventure at West Roxbury. It is profitless to speculate as to whether too much system killed the Phalanx, or whether the simple cohesion of the first Association might have averted any serious trouble. There is little doubt, however, that Albert Brisbane, despite his lofty and disinterested character, proved to be the evil genius of Brook Farm.[15]

Charles Fourier had created a theoretical utopia which is in the tradition of the hierarchical male fantasy utopias discussed in the previous chapters. While the communal life, good housing, and good food that he included are all positive aspects, their execution in his structured authoritarian system destroyed the very lifestyle they wish to create. This lonely and possibly crazy man created his own ideal, but when it was superimposed on an already successful experiment using feminist ideals at Brook Farm it helped to bring about the end of the experiment.

In a letter from Sophia Peabody (later married to Nathaniel Hawthorne) to Georgiana Kirby, Sophia described the difference between the original Brook Farm ideal and the Fourierism takeover which:

> frightened away the idealists whose presence had given to the spot its chief attraction and injured the pastoral bloom which beautified it. The reputation of Brook Farm for brilliancy, wit, and harmless eccentricity was seriously compromised. The joyous spirit of youth was sobered. The outside community henceforth regarded the enterprise as a mechanical attempt to reform society, rather than a poetic attempt to regenerate it.[16]

Herein lies the crux of the problem when abstract utopian thought is superimposed on a thriving community for political reasons. Here is a case where an egalitarian community is destroyed by outside forces which impose a hierarchical model on a working experiment. Possibly in the case of Brook Farm when it became the projection of Fourier, it lost its soul, its ethos.

Brook Farm is an example of how a philosophic ideal was put into reality in a working community as an "association of individuals." When the original ideal is ignored, the result can be disastrous as it was at Brook Farm. The idealist originators let an outside system which had an already structured utopian concept change the make-up and ethos of their community. From a cooperative Arcadian experiment they became a hierarchical experiment for artisans. A structured factory model of work was instituted, and the equal sharing feminist model was lost.

Meanwhile, a friend of Emerson, Bronson Alcott, also of Concord, decided to form a colony named Fruitlands, which only lasted from June to December of 1843, and was one of the more visionary schemes of the time. Like Brook Farm, which was located on poor farmland overlying gravel, Fruitlands was built on a beautiful piece of property with long views to the mountains of New Hampshire but had poor, rocky soil. It was located in the town of Harvard, Massachusetts which had harbored a successful five hundred member Shaker colony since 1793.

Fruitlands was another serious attempt to translate a philosophy into life in this case, the Transcendental philosophy. Property and money were eliminated, with Emerson acting as a trustee. Simplicity of diet, plain garments, and clean buildings were adopted. The members of the community were vegetarians, because they did not want to subjugate humans or beasts. They did not want to be "a cook and chambermaid to them three parts of the year. It was further felt that the eating of animal food tended to carnalize the spirit."[17] Fruitlands differed from Brook Farm in that it did not want to achieve an earthly utopia, but it instead intended to create a new sense of heaven in the individual soul. Its goal was individual and personal, not communal and sharing.

The reality of Fruitlands was that the only fruit was from a few barren apple trees, and Sarah Alcott (Bronson Alcott's wife and the only woman in the group) did most of the physical labor while the male philosophers sat around talking or traveled to solicit new recruits. Charles Lane, one of the founders, wanted to abolish marriage. Bronson Alcott was forced to choose between Lane representing "spirit" and his wife representing "family." Alcott chose family.

And what a family it was! Bronson Alcott is mainly known today as the father of Louisa May Alcott, the author of *Little Women*. The other daughters were artists and musicians. Alcott educated his own daughters and included them in his life whether it was walking with Thoreau or entertaining a fugitive slave at dinner. What he failed to accomplish in his utopian community, he accomplished with his family of women.

Fruitlands never grew beyond a community of fifteen members which consisted of Alcott and his family and the other people who were all male friends of his and Lane's. Since Lane bought the farm where Fruitlands was located, he attempted to be the controlling force. The dynamics were more like a joint partnership between Alcott and Lane with Mrs. Alcott as the only full-time employee who worked herself to exhaustion trying to cook and clean for fifteen people. When a visitor asked if there were any beasts of burden on the place, she replied, "Only one woman!"[18]

This experiment had the quality of a short-lived business venture or townspeople playing at a rustic life for a summer rather than a unifying community experiment. In the end Fruitlands came to nothing. "Alcott saw that the scornful words of Emerson were true—that it had been a very decent and innocent recreation, a kind of Puritan carnival."[19] The two male leaders had opposing needs: Lane to institute a celibate working community and Alcott to continue his life as a philosopher and family man. Sarah Alcott had her wealthy brother stop financially supporting Fruitlands when all the members except Lane left at the onset of winter, and her children and family were being negatively affected by the experiment. Lane joined the nearby Shaker community after Fruitlands collapsed.

Horace Mann, the first president of Antioch College, was also in the circle of the Transcendentalists, and was associated with Ellery Channing, Emerson, Nathaniel Hawthorne, and Bronson Alcott. Although both Mann and Alcott were contemporaries in educational reform, they were quite different. Mann was practical and would compromise while Alcott would not. Mann was successful in the outside world and was interested in results, while Alcott stood by his principles and was often unemployed. Alcott often asked himself the question put forth by Thoreau, "What can I do for which men will pay me?"[20]

Horace Mann, along with his second wife Mary Peabody Mann, carried many of the ideas of the Concord and Boston circle with them to Antioch College. Mary Peabody was the sister of Sophia Peabody, who had lived at Brook Farm and married Nathaniel Hawthorne. Hawthorne wrote the *Blithdale Romance* from his experiences at Brook Farm. Mary Peabody had also been in Ripley's congregation in Boston.

The difficulties of translating a philosophy such as Transcendentalism into a working community such as Fruitlands or Brook Farm are enormous. Living and thinking are two separate occupations. But when the ideal has an educational philosophy behind it, the founding idea or concept sometimes can be used to form a utopian educational institution. Fruitlands did not plan for a community which was equal and sharing. The men at Fruitlands accepted that they were in an extended paternalistic family where Mrs. Alcott was the "beast of burden" or mother and wife to them all.

Utopian colleges deal with the realities of life in a different manner. They must pay and provide for all menial services or have them shared equally. Antioch has a work/study program, usually off campus and career-oriented. World College West and Goddard both have a work program as part of the daily college life. The basic elements of life such as food and housing are usually provided in colleges, therefore eliminating many of the major causes of concern in communities and communes.

Another example of an American community experiment in the nineteenth century is Oneida which was founded in the early 1840's by a fanatical Christian, John Humphrey Noyes. Noyes first advocated male continence in the original community founded in the 1840's in Putney, Vermont. His first wife, Harriet Holton, lost four of the six children all born in the first six years of their marriage. Sympathetic to the teachings of Ann Lees, the leader of the Shakers, Noyes advocated celibacy for the same reason as she: the death of their children. The members of the Putney community were able to mingle freely between the sexes, as non sexual brothers and sisters, therefore eliminating the problem of unwanted pregnancy and childbirth deaths. Ironically, the local inhabitants of the town of Putney perceived the intermingling in the opposite way and lodged a bill of complaint against the community in the local court citing "adultery." The threat of mob violence caused the community to move to Oneida, near Buffalo, New York. In Oneida they struggled to exist until one of the members invented an improved steel trap, not unlike the proverbial "better mousetrap," which brought financial security to the commune. The community hired hundreds of outside people, built comfortable buildings, and also manufactured "Community Silver," a tableware used today. Unlike Brook Farm, artisans were an integral part of the Oneida community throughout its history.

After twenty years of abstinence, Noyes introduced intentional selective breeding at Oneida among 53 women and 38 men. The participants could turn down unwanted overtures, but needed the permission of the leaders to have sexual relations. Fifty-six children were subsequently born with John Noyes, now in his sixties, the father of eight of them. Noyes, influenced by Plato's *The Republic* and Campanella's *The City of The Sun,* was a eugenicist who put theory into practice. Women were considered as property, and as community property could be shared.

Although Oneida was financially successful, a group within the community organized against Noyes and his scientific breeding program. To avoid arrest Noyes crossed the border into Canada in June of 1879 and, on his advice, the community was turned into a joint-stock company. Oneida was a community which had trouble going from the "father figure" in the first generation to the second generation. The Oneida community is an example of how a paternalist society with sexist beliefs had difficulty going beyond the original family model. When the patriarch showed his human needs, the male leaders of the second generation questioned his ethics and then his leadership.

Sexist attitudes prevailed in many nineteenth century communities and were like Oneida where the commune reflected the desire of a charismatic leader to control others in the name of community welfare. For instance, one woman commented on the general hardships of New Harmony and wondered "if the prospect of paradise on earth were not a treachery played by the male imagination."[21] The dream and the reality conflicted sharply in nineteenth century utopian communities, not least of all in terms of life options available to women.

Translating the utopian dream of a college into reality often faces some of the difficulties found in community life in the nineteenth century communes. When a joint participation in utopian colleges between the faculty, administrators, and students is instituted, it often leads to a community spirit. The whole community usually restricts the power of any patriarch as did the Oneida community, if it is endangering the health of the group. Unfortunately, sometimes the dream and the reality in the utopian colleges are in conflict, as they were in the communities. But in some of the utopian colleges such as Goddard and formerly at World College West, community meetings brought out the concerns of each group to produce discussion and a solution in a circular way rather than the "top down" manner of management. When the hierarchical model prevails, the college leadership tends to become autocratic.

Another nineteenth century group, originated in the summer of 1874 at Chautauqua Lake in upstate New York, is interesting in light of similar experiments in non-residential education located at Goddard, Antioch, and The Union Institute. The Chautauqua movement spread to isolated communities throughout the Middle West and pioneered in correspondence courses, lecture-study groups, and reading circles.

Although the Chautauqua movement declined after World War I, it brought culture and education to the Midwest through non-residential courses and then throughout the United States in the last quarter of the nineteenth century. In the summer of 1997 C-Span carried a speech given before a large gathering at the Chautauqua headquarters in upper New York State.

The correspondence courses of the Chautauqua functioned in a similar style to the written, telephone, and electronic communication between a Goddard, Antioch, and The Union Institute non-residential learner and their core and adjunct faculty. The reading circles of the nineteenth century Middle West were usually women's literary groups as were so effectively described in the novel, ". . . *Ladies of the Club*" by Helen Hooven Santmyer. These circles functioned much as small seminar groups do, in a circular, non-hierarchical fashion. The lecture-study groups of the Chautauqua were closer to the traditional style of education, yet the residential components of the Chautauqua program were like the colloquiums and seminars of The Union Institute, Goddard, and Antioch.

As an outgrowth of the Methodist Church which originally planned to educate Sunday School teachers, the Chautauqua group was different from the other nineteenth century utopian communities in that it was a seasonal phenomena occurring only in summer. Maybe if Fruitlands had been planned as only a summer colony, it might have had a longer lifetime. Many Chautauquas still exist in the Midwest. I have visited one in southern Ohio and the one in Bay View, Michigan which is now functioning as a summer resort with cultural programs.

The educational tenets of the Chautauqua movement are apropos today. From a book published in 1885 is found the following quotation:

> Diversity in the direction of talent, and difference in degree, together with inequalities of social condition, may modify the demand upon the individual for culture and service; but the utter neglect of intellectual capacity is criminal, whether it be by menial or millionaire.[22]

In this book about the Chautauqua movement are many testimonies from students about their non-residential B.A. degree. Some are college age and taking the Chautauqua course along with their regular studies, for instance one was also a student at Williams College. Others write from California and throughout the United States while another writes from Oxford while studying in England. They are excited, committed students bent on self growth, and these accounts read like the accounts of students both adults and college age in the self-directed, non-residential courses of the utopian colleges today.

My favorite letter is from a woman who writes:

> I enjoy the C.L.S. very much. It gives me courage to feel, that, although I am forty-five years old, I am a scholar, and am in a school, and really learning something. My chance for school education was but little. After I was twelve years old, I stayed at home, and worked summers, and then had only three or four months of schooling in winter and for that I had to walk a mile and a half through unbroken snow roads. Do you wonder that C.L.S.C. comes to me like a God-given gift? Those that have been "scrimped" as I, can appreciate what it is to have a course of reading laid out for them. I do get discouraged at times when the work is hard, and I am so tired that I cannot understand what I am reading. I hope to go to Chautauqua for a week next summer. That seems to me to the nearest heaven I shall ever get on this earth.[23]

For this adult woman and many others like her, her "Heaven on Earth" was living and studying in her own home and briefly living at the temporal site of her educational experience.

After Chautauqua the communes, communities, and experiments in living that flourished in the United States in the nineteenth century subsided until they again sprung up in the 1960's. In the late 1960's and 1970's utopian experiments again arose in the United States and again reflected many of the same unrealized visions and tensions of the nineteenth century communes. Hundreds of groups came together to realize new ways of relating to each other and to the environment. Some developed out of the "hippie" culture and looked for rural settings to escape from American materialism. Their orientation might be religious, political, or environmental, or all three. They faced the same "issues of economic survival, relationship of individual to community, and how to achieve autonomy and new values troubled these groups as they had the nineteenth century experiments. They also reflect contemporary patterns in male/female relationships and male control of community structure."[24]

The utopian experiments of the sixties echo many of the concerns of earlier communities. Hugh Gardner in his study *Thirteen Modern American Communes* observed that there was continued sex-role specialization and comments on "patriarchal elements in almost all observed communes. Whatever the size, structure or values of the groups he examines, the thread of male superiority is evident."[25]

The dreams of an ideal future were present in the feminist creators of science fiction in the 1970's, but the life in the communes of the time was a far cry from the feminist utopias. But women have had a better chance in the utopian colleges where the issues of childrearing and household maintenance are not part of the lifestyle, and where women students and faculty have a chance for equality. But the utopian colleges often set up hierarchical structures which defeat their professed ideals.

Some of the best examples of long-lasting communal experiments are religious communal "experiments," such as the Christian and Buddhist ones which have lasted hundreds, almost thousands, of years. These communities usually are characterized by two qualities: They are oriented to something beyond themselves, in order to serve some purpose higher than themselves, and they are often highly authoritarian. This issue then brings us back to Socrates' question of the quality of leadership. If humans are to rule over other humans, what qualities must they possess? If a "heaven on earth" is to be attempted, must a human have a role of God?

After much thinking about these questions and others which arose from this line of thinking, my own human frailties and limitations became quite evident, along with the writers of utopias and the founders of communities and colleges. Ideals can be strived for, and hopes can be realized, but they will never fulfill the ideals or hopes of everyone.

The reality of this world is that life lives on life. All living beings on this planet must consume another living being to exist. "The big fish eats the little fish," and on and on, up and down the food chain. In a world with such a given set of principles, how can an ideal community exist in a less than ideal world?

Just as the chain of command of what eats what exists in this world, so does the reality of male power. Marilyn French writes about this reality as follows:

> And men have, through patriarchal forms, achieved power-in-the-world, men own 99 percent of the world's property and earn 90 percent of its wages, while producing only 55 percent of the world's food and performing only one-third of the world's work. Men rather exclusively direct the course not just of states and corporations but of culture; religion, arts, education. Despite the assaults of various waves of feminism, men have been able to retain their control over the people, creatures, plants, and even some of the elements of this planet. Many men wish to retain these powers.[26]

Things were not much better in 1991 when the United Nations released a report entitled, "The World's Women 1970–1990." It is the first global attempt to statistically measure women's place in society. The United Nations began its Decade for Women in 1975, but, even now, much of women's contribution "remains invisible or ignored" notes Joann Vaneck, a director of the project in the United Nations Statistical Office.[27]

According to various charts, the workplace almost everywhere around the globe is segregated by sex, with women generally in less prestigious and lower-paid jobs. Women work as much as men everywhere and an average of 13 hours more each week in Asia and Africa. The report's findings on leadership show that women are poorly represented in the ranks of power, policy, and decision-making, although they are found in large numbers in low-level positions of public administration, political parties, unions, and business.[28]

From a feminist point of view there is a desire for a more equitable system, a different culture. In the modern political and educational climate the utopian colleges often try to combine the positive qualities of the contemporary culture while attempting to remain economically viable. World College West with its high ideals and excellent international program was forced to close its doors. In terms of culture, the sixties through the present day communes were often identified with the counter culture, as are most of the utopian colleges which were examined. The utopian colleges became havens for political and social experiments which have lead American education in developing human equality. Not being restrictive in many of the ways of the American communes, such as following set rituals and cutting themselves off from the outside society, these utopian institutions have continued to dare to be different. The five colleges examined attempted to create an environment where many of the ills of our society were addressed and in many cases a utopian or better solution could be made. They have not always succeeded, and sometimes made the same mistakes found in the communities and communes. Sometimes the divergence between their dream and reality became the difference between a PR campaign and the daily difficulties of not always being able to live up to their own standard.

Notes

1 Erasmus, Charles J. *In Search of The Common Good: Utopian Experiments Past and Future.* Macmillan, The Free Press: New York, 1977, page 114.

2 Kephart, William M. *Extraordinary Groups: The Sociology of Unconventional Lifestyles.* St. Martin's Press: New York, 1976, page 283.

3 Ibid, p. 165.

4 Ibid, p. 165.

5 Ibid, p. 166.

6 Ibid, p. 168.

7 Cohne , Joseph H. *In Quest of Heaven: The Story of the Sunrise Co-operative Farm Community.* Porcupine Press: Philadelphia, 1975, page 13.

8 Orvis, Marianne (Dwight). *Letters from Brook Farm, 1944–1847.* Porcupine Press: Philadelphia, 1887, page 181.

9 Swift, Lindsay. *Brook Farm: Its Members, Scholars, and Visitors.* Corinth Books: New York, 1899, 1961. p. 270.

10 Ibid, p. 272.

11 Ibid, p. 277.

12 Ibid, p. 280.

13 Emerson, Ralph Waldo. *The Portable Emerson.* "Historic Notes of Life and Letters in New England." Penguin Books: New York, 1981, page 616.

14 Swift, Ibid, p. 280.

15 Ibid, p. 281.

16 Kirby, Georgiana Bruce. *Years of Experience: An Autobiographical Narrative.* AMS Press: New York, (1887), 1971, page 187.

17 McCuskey, Dorothy. *Bronson Alcott, Teacher.* Macmillan: New York, 1940, page 126.

18 Worthington, Marjorie. *Miss Alcott of Concord*, Doubleday & Co.: New York, 1958, p. 34.

19 Burton, Katherine. *Paradise Planters*, Longmans, Green & Co.: London, 1939, p. 111.

20 Ibid, p. 137.

21   Calverson, V. F. *Where Angels Dared to Tread*. Dobbs-Merrill, 1941. p. 191.

22   Vincent, John H. *The Chautauqua Movement*. Books for Libraries Press: Freeport, NY [1885], 1971, p. 2.

23   Ibid, p. 138.

24   Huckle, Patricia. "Women in Utopias." Sullivan, E.D.S. (ed). *The Utopian Vision: Seven Essays on the Quincentennial of Sir Thomas More*. San Diego State University Press; San Diego, CA. 1983, p. 123.

25   Ibid, p. 124.

26   French, Marilyn. *Beyond Power: On Women, Men, and Morals*. Summit books: New York, 1985. p. 231.

27   Howe, Marvine. "Sex Discrimination Persists, According to a U.N. Study," *The New York Times*, June 16, 1989.

28   Ibid.

Bibliography

1. Baylor, Ruth M. *Elizabeth Palmer Peabody: Kindergarten Pioneer.* University of Pennsylvania Press: Philadelphia, 1965.

2. Beecher, Jonathan and Bienvenu, Richard (ed.) *The Utopian Vision of Charles Fourier: Selected Texts on Work, Love and Passionate Attraction.* Beacon Press: Boston, 1971.

3. Burton, Katherine. *Paradise Planters,* Longmans, Green & Co.: London, *1939.*

4. Calverson, V. F. *Where Angels Dared to Tread.* Dobbs-Merrill: New York, 1941.

5. Carden, Maren. Lockwood. *Oneida: Utopian Community to Modern Corporation.* The Johns Hopkins Press: Baltimore, Maryland, 1969.

6. Codman, John Thomas. *Brook Farm: Historic and Personal Memoirs.* Arena Publishing Co.: Boston, MA. 1894

7. Cohne, Joseph J. *In Quest of Heaven: The Story of the Sunrise Co-operative Farm Community.* Porcupine Press: Philadelphia, 1975.

8. Darin-Drabkin, Dr. H. *The Other Society.* Harcourt, Brace & World: New York, 1961.

9. Downs, Robert B. *Horace Mann: Champion of Public Schools.* Twayne Publishers, NY, 1977.

10. Emerson, Ralph Waldo. *The Portable Emerson.* "Historic Notes of Life and Letters in New England." Penguin Books: New York, 1981.

11. Erasmus, Charles J. *In Search of the Common Good: Utopian Experiments Past and Future.* MacMillian, The Free Press: New York, 1977.

12 French, Marilyn. *Beyond Power: On Women, Men, and Morals.* Summit Books: New York, 1985. p. 531.

13. Gould, Joseph E. *The Chautauqua Movement.*, State University of New York: Albany, NY, 1961.

14. Hien, Robert V. *California's Utopian Colonies.* Yale University Press: New Haven, 1966.

15. Huckle, Patricia. "Women in Utopies." Sullivan, E.D.S. (ed). *The Utopian Vision: Seven Essays on the Quincentennial of Sir Thomas More.* San Diego State University Press: San Diego, CA. 1983.

16. *Ideal Commonwealths: Plutarch's Lycurgus, More's Utopia, Bacon's New Atlantic, Campanella's City of the Sun.* With an introduction by Henry Morley. Routledge: London, 1885.

17. Kanter, Rosabeth Moss. *Commitment and Community: Communes and Utopias in Sociological Perspective.* Harvard University Press: Cambridge, MA. 1972, p. 75.

18. Kephart, William M. *Extraordinary Groups: The Sociology of Unconventional Lifestyles.* St. Martin's Press: New York, 1976.

19. Kirby, Georgiana Bruce. *Years of Experience. An Autobiographical Narrative.* AMS Press: New York [1887], 1971.

20. Manuel, Frank E. and Fritzie P. *Utopian Thought in the Western World.* The Belknap Press of Harvard University Press: Cambridge, MA., 1980.

21. McCuskey, Dorothy. *Bronson Alcott, Teacher.* Macmillan: New York, 1940.

22. Messerli, Jonathan. *Horace Mann: A Biography.* Alfred A. Knopf: New York, 1972.

23. *Modern Man in Search of Utopia.* San Francisco Alternatives Foundation, 1971.

24. More, Sir Thomas. *Utopia.* Ed. Collins, J. Churton. Oxford University Press: London, 1961.

25. Mumford, Lewis. *The Story of Utopias.* With an introduction by Hendrik Willem Van Loon. Smith: Gloucester, MA., 1959.

26. Noyes, John Humphrey. *History of American Socialisms.* J. B. Lippincott: Philadelphia, 1870.

27. Nordoff, Charles. *The Communistic Societies of The United States.* Harper and Brothers: New York, 1875.

28. Orvis, Marianne Dwight. *Letters from Brook Farm: 1844–1847.* Porcupine Press: Philadelphia, 1972. Also Vassar College: Poughkeepsie: NY, 1928.

29. Owen, Robert. *The Book of the New Moral World.* Augustus M. Kelley: New York [1842], 1970.

30. Ozmon, Howard. *Utopias and Education.* Burgess Publishing Co., 1969.

31. Parker, Robert Allerton. *A Yankee Saint: John Humphrey Noyes and the Oneida Community.* Porcupine Press, Inc.: Philadelphia, 1972.

32. Plato. *The Republic.* Modern Library: New York, 1982.

33. Plattel, Martin G. *Utopian and Critical Thinking.* Duquesne University Press: Pittsburgh, PA, 1972.

34. Randall, E.O. *History of The Zoar Society: A Sociological Study in Communism.* Press of Fred J. Herr, 1904.

35. Richter, Peyton B. (ed.). *Utopias: Social Ideals and Communal Experiments.* Holbrook Press, Inc.: Boston, 1971.

36. *Robert Owen and His Social Philosophy.* AMS Press: New York, [1860], 1971.

37. Robertson, Constance Noyes. *Oneida Community Profiles.* Syracuse University Press, 1977.

38. Sams, Henry W. (Editor) *Autobiography of Brook Farm.* Prentice-Hall: Englewood Cliffs, NJ, 1958.

39. Sears, Clara Endicott. *Bronson Alcott's Fruitlands.* Houghton Mifflin & Co.: Boston, 1915.

40. Spencer, M.C. *Charles Fourier.* Twayne Publishers: Boston, MA, 1981.

41. Swift, Lindsay. *Brook Farm: Its Members, Scholars, and Visitors.* Corinth Books: New York, 1961.

42. Tharp, Louise Hall. *Until Victory: Horace Mann and Mary Peabody.* Little, Brown and Company: Boston, 1953.

43. *Utopian Studies 1.* Edited by Beauchamp, Gorman, Roemer, Kenneth, Smith, Nicholas D. University Press of America: New York, 1987.

44. Vincent, John H. *The Chautauqua Movement.* Books for Libraries Press: Freeport, NY [1883], 1971.

45. Williams, E.I.F. *Horace Mann: Educational Statesman.* The Macmillan Co.: New York, 1937.

46. Worthington, Marjorie. *Miss Alcott of Concord,* Doubleday & Co.: New York, 1958.

Chapter 4

A Brief Overview of American Higher Education, Robber Barons, and the Progressive Movement

In this chapter a overview of three seemingly disparate subjects, American higher education, robber barons, and the progressive movement, will be briefly discussed to reflect the change in the United States from a rural society to an industrialized one, especially at the end of the nineteenth century. Traditional American higher education was an outgrowth and a reflection of various cultural and economic trends, and as such made the transition in the nineteenth century from small private colleges for the sons of the wealthy to state-supported institutions which utilized the factory model of higher education. This factory model was an outgrowth of the utility model of higher education which was instituted in the mining and agricultural colleges which were used to expand the frontier. The factory and utility models of education were the dominant, and still are, models of American higher education. While this type of education promoting the economic and business growth of the United States prevails, other forms of education were introduced by the progressive movement. When the robber barons helped to issue in the twentieth century which has been dominated by big business in the United States, small pockets of experimental education already existed. But later in the 1920's at Antioch Arthur Morgan was able to combine business practices of a more entrepreneurial nature into the fabric of an experimental education which was individualistic, not hierarchical as in the standard corporate business structure.

Alongside the prevailing cultural, economic, and educational forces in American higher education, another type of education began at

Antioch in the mid-1850's and continues to this day. This type of education was utopian in concept and often in practice. Forward thinking ideas prevailed at this and other utopian colleges, and later their ideas were often incorporated into mainstream American higher education. But without the small classes and the intensity of the teaching which are part of the utopian model, the ideas were often diluted or lost in the factory style of education.

The American utopian communities which thrived in the utopian thinking and frontier expansion days of the mid-nineteenth century died out at the same time the robber barons helped to change the United States from a rural economy to an industrialized one. The utopian communities only existed in isolated pockets during the twentieth century until the nineteen-sixties and seventies when the counterculture moved against the materialistic way of life in America and again set up alternate lifestyles in communes. But both the American utopian communities and published utopias of the time were separate from the course of mainstream American higher education in both the nineteenth and twentieth centuries, while the utopian communities instead paralleled the cycles of expansion and growth in the utopian colleges which dealt with experimental and progressive ideas.

In his history of the era between the Civil War and the end of the nineteenth century, Matthew Josephson described the robber barons.

> The members of this new ruling class were generally, and quite aptly, called "barons," "kings," "empire-builders," or even "emperors." They were aggressive men, as were the first feudal barons; sometimes they were lawless; in important crises, nearly all of then them tended to act without those established moral principles which fixed more or less the conduct of the common people of the community. '. . . These men were robber barons as were their medieval counterparts, the dominating figures of an aggressive economic age.'

The robber barons and others heavily influenced American economic life during the last part of the nineteenth century when the utopian colonies were fading. Bellamy's book, *Looking Backward*, is a utopian response to the inequities of this era. From a rural, or Arcadian, lifestyle to a capitalistic and industrial age, American life was heavily influenced by this group of American industrialists called "robber barons." But what do robber barons have to do with utopian colleges? But they are significant, since their thought and money have heavily influenced traditional American higher education in the twentieth century while John Dewey's progressive thought has influenced the utopian colleges.

This "aggressive economic age" from the 1890's to the 1920's gave a new economic system carved from the vast natural storehouse of American forests, coal, oil, with the transportation vehicles of railroads and ships. From the fortunes of these men also came many educational structures which influenced twentieth-century American higher education. The Carnegie Foundation, Vanderbilt University, and The Rockefeller Foundation are just a few of these robber baron names which are now attached to public and private institutions. Josephson characterized these men and their times when he wrote: "When the group of men arose who formed the subject of this history, the United States was a mercantile-agrarian democracy. When they departed or retired from active life, it was something else: a unified industrial society, the effective economic control of which was lodged in the hands of a hierarchy."[2]

A factory system had replaced an agrarian system which in turn influenced American higher education. The colleges originated in the agrarian-mercantile era of American history which ran from the founding of the United States until the time of the robber barons were usually for the upper classes and produced ministers, scholars, and statesmen, although no mention was made of stateswomen, some must have existed. They were ivory towers which did not educate the workers, artisans, and "common folk." When the land grant colleges, utility schools, and public higher education were introduced, American higher education fell mostly into the hands of American business which rules it to the present. Cost-effectiveness and bottom-line business thinking prevail at American traditional universities, and students, faculty, and administrators are arranged in a hierarchical corporate structure. Higher education has become big business in both philosophy and action. Business schools, medical schools, and other money-making departments of the large research universities dominate mainstream higher education.

An example of a robber baron was Andrew Carnegie, who was the founder of the Carnegie Foundation for The Advancement of Teaching. The Carnegie Foundation continues today to play a critical role in United States education, and as such is an example of the relationship between the hierarchy of capitalistic wealth and its influence on contemporary American education. The period from 1890–1920 which marked the transition from the earlier individualistic competitive structure in business to its contemporary corporate form is similar to the period of the late sixties and early seventies.[3] Carnegie in the period

1890–1920 personally responded to the breakdown of his hierarchical control over the people working for him by calling against them the National Guard, trainloads of strikebreakers, and his Pinkerton men.[4]

The domination of the capitalistic power elite over the people had been voiced earlier by Horace Mann, the first president of Antioch, when he in 1842, as the then secretary of the Massachusetts State Board of Education and the most prominent educational reformer of the nineteenth century, said:

> Nothing but universal education can counter work this tendency to the domination of capital and the servility of labor. If one class possesses all of the wealth and education, while the residue of society is ignorant and poor . . . the latter in fact and in truth, will be the servile dependents and subjects of the former.[5]

What Mann did not foresee was the opportunity for universal education preparing students in the factory model of education. While most of twentieth century American higher education was available for all, the system of education was constructed along the lines of the hierarchical American corporation which keeps the power and money in the hands of a few.

At the end of the nineteenth century the utopian idea was still partially alive through the Bellamy societies springing up throughout the country using *Looking Backward* as a blueprint for the future. Horace Mann had brought public education to all on the high school level. Sophia Peabody had begun a kindergarten as a model for future generations. But the factory system of business which had fueled the nineteenth century common-school movement to create primary education for the masses was continued into higher education where the model was much the same. Then the change from the nineteenth century entrepreneurial business system was transferred to the twentieth century corporate model. In the twentieth century corporate expansion continued to grow to its present multinational state. The factory model with a corporate system became the higher education model for American education growing from the utility model of mining and agricultural colleges used to expand the frontier.

Most liberal arts institutions in the United States were grounded in the traditions of the European institutions of Oxford and Cambridge. For the first two centuries of American educational history class distinctions and the use of child labor made higher education the privi-

lege of the few despite the effects of the American revolution. Religious intolerance from the Puritans was the order of the day with
many religious splinter groups starting their own colleges in much the
same way as the utopian communities began. Colleges multiplied three-
fold within ten years after the Revolutionary War, but they were small
and conservative. The colleges were remote from life and educated
only young men, since women were barred. Most schools were formal
and had a mechanical character. The English college became the
American university with a graduate school borrowed from Germany.[6]
Oberlin had opened up its classes to women in 1838, but it was not
until 1853 that Antioch made them full, functioning, and equal members of the college community. Many of the women attending Oberlin
at that time transferred to Antioch where they could receive a co-
educational experience of living in dormitories, eating, and attending
classes as the equal of male students.

But at the end of the nineteenth century an educational philosopher, John Dewey, created a "progressive," or what I see as "utopian," system of education which was in contrast to the traditional
American higher education system, or the utilitarian model. With educational roots from philosophy, or "utopian thinking," not from institutions used to educate the upper classes or business or state supported higher education based on the factory model, Dewey developed
an educational model which is still used today in the "utopian
colleges."

John Dewey, who had come from the same New England tradition
as Ralph Waldo Emerson and William James, grew up in a small town
in Vermont. Dewey as a village dweller, had the same idealized, but
not practical, view of farming as many other townspeople and utopian
community founders. He attended public school and at Johns Hopkins
developed his career direction of becoming a philosopher. Throughout his life Dewey continued to find Plato the most stimulating of "the
bearers of the ceaseless enterprise which is philosophy."[7] Dewey taught
at the University of Michigan and the University of Minnesota before
going to the new University of Chicago. This move and his reading of
William James's, *Principles of Psychology,* were important influences
upon his pragmatic philosophy of education. He was fifty-seven years
old when he published the summation of his educational philosophy,
Democracy and Education, in 1916.[8]

As one of the most original of American educational philosophers,
Dewey observed that education can foster personal development and

economic equality while integrating youth into adult society only under one condition: a thorough extension of democracy to all parts of the social order.[9] He believed that economic justice is built on a society of individuals capable of interpersonal relationships on the basis of equality and reciprocity. Dewey's ideal society and a truly utopian society or college can only occur when all relationships of power and authority are based on equal participation and consent. Unfortunately, contradictory forces prevail in our society. The economic and social elites of the United States have sought to use the educational system as a way to produce profitable types of business behavior reflected in our society.

But a utopian college appeals to a different type of person. In contrast to a purely job oriented education, a utopian education ideally brings together all aspects of the human experience to educate a morally healthy person of conscience. Horace Mann tried to instill the idea of this type of person into his educational philosophy exercised at Antioch during his tenure as their first president. John Dewey in his tenets of progressive education believes in the whole person, not just a job robot trained to follow orders. Dewey's educational philosophy was directly applied at Goddard by Royce Pitkin and by other utopian college educators.

John Dewey was aware of the effect of the culture on education and that the culture would replicate itself in the educational system. He wrote that: "To transmute a society built on an industry which is not yet humanized into a society which wields its knowledge and its industrial power in behalf of a democratic culture requires the courage of an inspired imagination."[10] But Dewey believed that the two could be combined. The challenge of education in the twentieth century was to either combine or exclude the culture. The exclusive universities tried to broaden their base with more liberalized admission policies in response to the dominate culture while the public institutions did the same on a larger scale. After World War I the economic structure needed more educated workers even though most of the work was in the factory and with machines. The idea of a democratic education to educate students for a democratic society which meant sharing was new when introduced by Dewey. He pointed towards a one-class society which he based on the family model of self-sufficiency which he probably observed in his boyhood in Vermont. But in reality the family model is often patriarchal, not truly one-class.

But Dewey felt that thinking was the primary means of growth and as such can be learned by male or female, child or adult. Thinking begins with problem solving, he felt, and therefore Dewey tended to select problems which lead to immediate action. He wanted concrete results and suspected truths that cannot be observed at once. He was not as interested in traditional science as with the science of living which he felt makes life safe, healthful, intelligent, and positive. His ideas of progressive education can be seen in all of the utopian colleges studied.

Meanwhile, during the first half of the twentieth century a discussion among educators swung between the proponents of the German research system of education and the English educational system that "valued character and administrative ability more highly than technical scholarship."[11] Robert Hutchins and Abraham Flexer kept this argument alive. Hutchins accepted the research function of the university, but by "research" he meant mainly philosophic reflection with logic as its main instrument, with a base of Platonic ideas and intuition. In *No Friendly Voice: Higher Learning in America* (1936) and *Conflict in Education in a Democratic Society*, (1953) Hutchins further expounded his educational ideas. He began the University of Chicago school of education with a curriculum built around great books, although John Ershine, a Columbia professor, gave the first "great books" course at Columbia University, and this model of education had been used previously at St. John's College, Maryland and many adult education centers.[12]

A type of utopian experiment was formed by Alexander Meiklejohn in an Experimental College at the University of Wisconsin between 1927 and 1932. This college was open only to men even though it was located at a coed university which made it seem like a step back to me while ideologically purporting to be both experimental and forward thinking. The freshman year offered a study of ancient Greek education, and in the sophomore year the students compared Greek with modern American civilization. The students lived in a separate building, and the plan was expensive. The university ended this costly experiment after five years for economic reasons. This college did not follow the criteria used for the five colleges examined, since it contained the single sex (male) model and based its curriculum exclusively on the Western tradition.

In this brief look at American higher education, we see that Hutchins and Meiklejohn exposed problems which are surfacing again in education today. The debate between the large research universities stressing scientific research vs. the liberal arts with active teaching is still heard. But as avant-garde as Meiklejohn may have seemed, his Experimental College excluded women. In contrast, the utopian colleges have attempted to use the basic tenets of progressive education, and all are dedicated to equality both in theory and in practice. From the colonial days of American higher education to the present, mainstream colleges have reflected the prevailing economic and cultural American trends while the utopian colleges thrived during times of counterculture views.

Notes

1   Josephson, Matthew. *The Robber Barons: The Great American Capitalists, 1861–1901*. Harcourt, Brace and Company: New York, 1934. p. vii (Forward).

2   Ibid, p. vii.

3   U.S. Department of Labor, *Monthly Labor Review,* September, 1974, p. 50.

4   Bowles, Samuel and Ginitis, Herbert. *Schooling in Capitalist America: Educational Reform and The Contradictions of Economic Life.* Basic Books: New York, 1976. p. 180.

5   Ibid, p. 24.

6   Good, H.G. *A History of American Education.* The Macmillan Company: New York, 1956. p. 353.

7   Ibid, p. 356.

8   Ibid, p. 357.

9   Dewey, John A. *Democracy and Education.* The Free Press; New York, 1966. p. 20.

10   Dewey, John. "American Education and Culture," *John Dewey on Education.* Random House: New York, 1964. p. 291.

11   Good, p. 482.

12   Ibid, p. 480.

Bibliography

1. Adler, Mortimer J. *Reforming Education: The Opening of the American Mind*. Collier Books: New York, 1988.

2. Aldrich, Nelson W., Jr. *Old Money: The Mythology of America's Upper Class*. Alfred A. Knopf: New York, 1988.

3. *Barron's Profiles of American Colleges: Descriptions of the Colleges*. Sixteenth Edition, New York: Barron's Educational Series, 1988.

4. Barzun, Jacques. *The American University: How it runs, Where it is going*. Harper & Row: New York, 1968.

5. Bear, John, Ph.D. *Bear's Guide to Earning Non-Traditional College Degrees*. Ten Speed Press: Berkeley, 1988.

6. Bender, Thomas. (Editor) *The University and the City From Medieval Origins to the Present*. Oxford University Press: New York, Oxford, 1988.

7. Bloom, Allan. *The Closing of the American Mind*. Simon & Schuster: New York, 1987.

8. Bowles, Samuel and Gintis, Herbert. *Schooling in Capitalist America: Educational Reform and the Contradictions of Economic Life*. New York: Basic Books, 1976.

9. Brubacher, John S. and Rudy, Willis. *Higher Education in Transition. A history of American colleges and Universities 1636–1976*. Harper & Row, Publishers: 1958, 1976.

10. Clark, Burton R. *The Higher Education System; Academic Organization in Cross-National Perspective*. University of California Press: Berkeley, 1983.

11. Clark, Burton R. *The School and the University: An International Perspective*. University of California Press: Berkeley, 1985.

12. Counts, George S. *The American Road to Culture: A Social Interpretation of Education in the United States*. The John Day Co.: New York, 1930.

13. Cremin, Lawrence A. *Popular Education and Its Discontents*. Harper & Row: New York, 1989.

14. Dewey, John. *American Education and Culture*. New York, 1964.

15. Dewey, John A. *Democracy and Education*. The Free Press: New York, 1966.

16. Dewey, John. *John Dewey on Education*. Selected Writings. Edited and with an introduction by Reginald D. Archambault. Modern Library: New York, 1964.

17. Dewey, John. *Moral Principles in Education.* Southern Illinois University Press: Carbondale, 1975.

18. Gardner, Ralph, Jr. *Young, Gifted, & Rich.* Simon & Schuster: New York, 1984.

19. Good, H.G. *A History of American Education.* The Macmillan Co: New York, 1956.

20. Harris, Raymond P. *American Education: Facts, Fancies, and Folklore.* Random House: New York, 1961.

21. Heilbroner, Robert L. *The Worldly Philosophers.* Simon & Schuster: New York, 1953.

22. Hughes, James Monroe. *Education in America.* Harper & Row: New York

23. Hutchins, Robert Maynard. *The Higher Learning in America.* Yale University Press: New Haven, 1936.

24. Josephson, Matthew. *The Robber Barons: The Great American Capitalists, 1861–1901.* Harcourt, Brace and Company: New York, 1934.

25. Myers, Gustavus. *History of the Great American Fortunes.* The Modern Library: New York, 1907.

26. Power, Edward J. *Education for American Democracy: Foundation of Education.* McGraw-Hill: New York, 1965.

27. Rudolph, Frederick. *The American College and University.* Alfred A. Knopf: New York, 1962.

28. *Top American Colleges*, compiled and edited by The College Research Group of Concord, Massachusetts, New York: Pocket Books, 1988.

29. Tewksbury, Donald G. *The Founding of American Colleges and Universities Before the Civil Way: With Particular Reference to the Religious Influences Bearing Upon the College Movement.* Archon Books/Teachers College, Columbia University: New York, 1932, 1965.

30. U.S. Department of Labor, Monthly Labor Review, September, 1974.

Chapter 5

Generational, Feminist, and Cultural Cycles in Relation to Utopian Colleges

In this chapter rudimentary thoughts are expressed with the hope that in the future some sociologist will take these seeds of ideas and test their validity and expand upon the premises which are only suggested. The three generation model of the life of an enterprise is only suggested in the most general form. Hopefully, some successive writer, or myself in a future project, can research, document, and expand this model more extensively. As it stands now, it is only an untested theory of the correlation between the feminist and cultural cycles to the same times at utopian colleges. Maybe this chapter should have been removed, but the author felt a "germ of a truth" was contained in it and, therefore, kept it in this book. But the reader must accept the fact the ideas are neither fully examined nor are they much more than "hunches."

The difference between what I refer to as utopian colleges and the traditional educational system becomes more apparent in the twentieth century. Both the American economic system and the educational system went through a change from 1890 to 1920. Farming was less important, and the concept of the whole family working together on the farm almost disappeared. Many of the rural utopian societies of the nineteenth century were largely built on the patriarchal model and were agriculturally based. They often dissolved when the "founding father" lost control and did not survive into a second or third generation.

In order for a utopian college to survive, it is helpful to have an ideological dream that encourages financial stability beyond the first generation. The first generation usually has a charismatic leader who has an idea and brings this idea into reality through hard work and intelligent business moves. Often the first generation is the time of dreams turning into buildings, as with the Oneida community which was an example of how the first generation worked in both a familial and business sense.

But before the building and the products had to come the vision.. All of the utopias from Plato to Hutchins were plans for a better society than the then existing one. Plato envisioned a society in which education was available to all, but he felt that shoemakers should be trained as shoemakers, not philosophers. He did not conceive of a shoemaker-philosopher in his stratified society. Bellamy was so convinced that his citizen army would be harmonious that he did not question the hierarchical system which seems to be the basis of any army whether it be citizen or not. Many of the written utopias from Plato through More to Bellamy attacked the material inequities, but they did not remove many of the basic thought patterns which again structured a society on a hierarchical system. In my opinion, a utopian model would be more equal and co-operative, not hierarchical.

But returning to the three generation theory where sometimes the second generation of a business, family, or business family does not have a drive for success. They do not have to work as hard, since they are carrying out someone else's dream, not their own. They often have more leisure for either more education and culture or for dissipation and trouble making. This generation can go either way: it can continue to strive for realizing the ideal or can become the "idle rich."

The third generation inherits both the dream and the fruits of their parents and grandparent's work. Often this is the generation of the "greedy heirs" who want to inherit what they have not worked for, but they wish to maintain a lifestyle to which they have become accustomed. They criticize, but do not invent. They accept their lifestyle as their just due, but are unwilling to sacrifice for it. They often squander the original fortune and find themselves in shirtsleeves again. But sometimes some members of the third generation have a respect for the founders and have a historical point of view and a work ethic which carries on the original vision.

In a business the generational model is similar. The original creator of the vision works hard until the dream is realized. This dream may produce a product or another way of manipulating money or a variety of different ways to create a successful material goal. The first generation makes the dream a reality. The second business generation carries out the dream, often taking it nationwide or worldwide. The employees, who knew the founder and believe in the original business concept, are usually working for a salary, not for visionary goals. They are ranked as to their worth by how much stock they own or how much they are paid. The hierarchical structure moves firmly in place.

The third generation often loses the original concept or vision. The founder is now either dead or ineffectual and as the "greedy heirs," the third generation fights with their siblings and co-workers over what they think should belong to them. They often do not have the drive to continue the original dream, but only look after their own interests. The generational pattern sometimes moves this generation to look back at the first generation and begin over again.

The corporate model, which began in the twentieth century, is also based on the patriarchal and hierarchical models. The patriarch or president may be benevolent or despotic, but the structure remains the same: all power resides in his hands. In a matriarchy the functions are the same as in a patriarchy, since the hierarchical system just places a female rather than a male in the position of power. A woman can be as tyrannical a leader as a man. The corporate model is a pyramid with all the power going from the top down.

The dream for a communal, sharing experience runs through most of the utopias, but in the utopian communities a hierarchical structure often emerges as the community grows larger or moves into a second generation. Leaders want to share, until someone does not agree with them. Writers want to create a perfect world for themselves, but probably could not live in it. Community experiments start with harmony, but often fall apart with disagreements among the members. Utopian communal living is difficult for the individual. Thoreau lived a "utopian life," but he had trouble in his interpersonal relationships.

An example of the difficulty of living in a utopian community was Bronson Alcott. He had only a sixth grade education, but started and ran his own school. His experiment in utopian living at Fruitlands was considered a failure. One of the reasons for this failure was that he relied on his wife to do most of the physical labor for not only his immediate family, but the other fifteen members of the community. When Charles Lane pitted him against his wife and children and wanted him to adopt a celibate life while ignoring his family, he refused. But the ultimate end of Fruitlands occurred when Alcott's wife Sarah told her wealthy brother, Sam May, not to continue supporting the experiment. Economics again determined the future of a utopian experiment. Bronson Alcott then reverted to the family structure rather than the communal one. Both individuals and families have trouble within the communal experience.[1]

Residential utopian colleges, on the other hand, allow individuals to leave their family structure for a communal college experience. Even in the institutions (Goddard, Antioch, and Union) where an individual is allowed to continue their own life and remain with their own family, as in the Chautauqua experiment, they often adhere to the utopian ideals of the education which they are acquiring.

During the twentieth century the American culture and external events continued to influence the course of higher education in the United States. Utopian colleges sprung up and thrived in the 1920's and 1960's. Antioch gained a new direction in the twenties while Sarah Lawrence was founded, and in the sixties, The Union Institute, World College West, Hampshire College, and others sprung to life. Goddard and Antioch saw their greatest expansion and acceptance during the sixties and seventies. Utopian colleges seem to spring up in the times of optimist utopian thinking and planning for a better future.

Utopian colleges often grew during periods of feminist revolt and declined during times of reactionary thought which excluded or contained women, such as in the decades of the 1950's and 1980's. When women are allowed to be heard and are valued in society, utopian colleges also are allowed to educate in a humane, not warlike or corporate model, way. In a loose overview of the history of feminism over the last 150 years, there were three peaks of activity: a first peaking in the 1850's; a second in the period 1900–1920; and a third peak beginning in the late 1960's. Alice S. Rossi, a professor of sociology, noticed this generational pattern in her essay in *The Feminist Papers: From Adams to de Beauvoir* when she wrote: "An alternating generational phenomenon is suggested in this dialectic pattern, with the feminist impulse acted out publicly in one generation and more privately in the next."[2] She goes on to write that the late 1870's and 1880's were times of great expansion in women's higher education and in white-collar clerical and professional jobs for women. She thinks that the daughters of the 1850's activists might have become directed towards private education and employment while moving away from political activity and public visibility. The daughters of the suffragists did the same in the 1930's. But ironically, during the thirties when feminism was supposedly dead, women earned the highest proportion of advanced degrees in the history of American higher education.[3] Maybe the general culture allows women to gain advanced degrees when it is consumed with its own financial woes. Usually women are only able to indulge in political activity as an extracurricular activity above the responsibilities of work and family, therefore the descendants of the women of Susan Anthony's and Elizabeth Stanton's generation were working and raising families. The same was true of the generation after the suffragists and the present generation of post feminists.

Depression and war are supposed to be "bad times" for women as with the rest of society, but exceptions to the rule, as in the above case can happen. During times of economic stress the pressure used to be for "one job per family," so that the limited amount of work could be spread around.[4] But in the nineteen eighties, a time of national expansion, the "feminization of poverty" was the rule when multiple families and serial marriages left many women as the head of a financially destitute family unit.

War causes another social flux when the women assume the "Rosie the Riveter" roles when the men are gone, but are expected to be exclusively wives and mothers when the soldiers return. People mobilize with a great energy in public and national service during a time of emergency, but retreat to private lives at war's end. The patterns of the Korean war, Vietnam war, and the Gulf war have caused different living patterns, since they did not take away a whole generation of men as did World War I and II.

Professor Rossi wrote:

> If sons forget what grandsons wish to remember, perhaps daughters, too, forget what granddaughters wish to remember. The striving second generation may struggle for status while the third generation seeks to recapture the thirst for freedom or social justice or women's rights of the first generation. Many early abolitionists in the 1830's were the grandchildren of Revolutionary soldiers, and today [1970's] many young feminists may be the granddaughters of the suffragists and radical reformers who made their mark early in the twentieth century. The quiet second generation, unnoted by historians, may consolidate gains, and provide the foundation on which the third generation takes off again into public and historical notice.[5]

If both feminist and cultural generational cycles have the same cycles as utopian or experimental education in the United States, is it too far fetched to think that these educational ideas and institutions could be havens for feminist thinking and leaders who are non-sexist?

Harold Taylor, as president of Sarah Lawrence College, wrote in 1953 in a chapter, "On The Education of Women," in his book, *On Education and Freedom,* that:

The particular questions to be raised about the education of women raise all the other questions of modern life. They cannot be answered by assigning women to a role decided upon by a combination of cultured habit and masculine prejudice. We have to remember that there is no ultimate purpose in liberal education beyond that of learning to live a complete life to the limit of its personal, social, spiritual, and physical dimension.[6]

Utopian colleges need not be exclusive to one gender, but must imbue the equal seeking for individual growth and education. A utopian college does not need the chain of command of an army or a business corporation, but instead should contain individuals and groups which cooperate in a "think tank" and mutually cooperative manner which is creative and not ego driven. Utopian colleges which are used as laboratories of learning that can be transferred to the general American culture are as important as large medical schools. The human spirit could also be supported, because it is as important as experiments for the human body such as cancer research and biotech marvels. As John Dewey thought, the science of living is as important, or more so, than traditional science.

Page Smith in his book, *Killing the Spirit*, wrote: "Thus, I suspect, the morale of women students is, generally speaking, much better than the morale of their male counterparts. They are the last utopians; they have revived the dream of a better, more humane society, not to be achieved this time by science or reason or objectivity, but by the keener sensibilities and nobler character of women."[7]

The generational and feminist cycles are worth examining, and a more exhaustive study than the brief treatment in this chapter should be devoted to it. The question of feminist revolt followed by reactionary thought cycles could be analyzed along with the cycles of war, depression, and politics in American society. How do they all relate to utopian thinking and eventually to utopian education? Where do the cycles overlap and where do they diverge? Why? Hopefully, in a future project, someone can find more evidence and data than the limited examples contained in this chapter.

Notes

1   Clara Endicott Sears, ed. *Bronson Alcott's Fruitlands*. Houghton Mifflin Co.: Boston, 1915.

2   Rossi, Alice S. *The Feminist Papers: From Adams to de Beauvoir*. Columbia University Press: New York and London, 1973. p. 616.

3   Ibid, p. 617.

4   Ibid, p. 617.

5   Ibid, p. 619.

6   Taylor, Harold. "On the Education of Women" *On Education and Freedom*. Southern Illinois University Press: Feffer & Simons, Inc.: London and Amsterdam, 1954, 1967, p. 203.

7   Smith, Page. *Killing the Spirit: Higher Education in America*. Viking: New York, 1990. p. 292.

Bibliography

1. Anderson, Scarvia B. *Sex Differences and Discrimination in Education.* Charles A. Jones Publishing Co.: Worthington, Ohio, 1971.

2. Bellah, Robert Neeley. *Habits of the Heart: Individualism and Commitment in American Life.* University of California Press: Berkeley, 1985.

3. Gezi, Kalil I. *Teaching in American Culture.* Holt, Rinehart and Winston: New York, 1968

4. Minnich, Elizabeth Kamarck, *Transforming Knowledge.* Temple University Press: Philadelphia, PA, 1990.

5. Noddings, Nel. *Caring: A Feminine Approach to Ethics and Moral Education.* University of California Press: Berkeley, 1984.

6. Rossi, Alice S. *The Feminist Papers: From Adams to de Beauvoir.* Columbia University Press: New York and London, 1973.

7. Sears, Clara Endicott, ed. *Bronson Alcott's Fruitlands.* Houghton Mifflin Co.: Boston, 1915.

8. Sexton, Patricia. *Women in Education.* Phi Delta Kappa Educational Foundation. Bloomington, Indiana, 1976.

9. Smith, Page. *Killing the Spirit: Higher Education in America.* Viking: New York, 1990.

10. Taylor, Harold. "On the Education of Women," *On Education and Freedom.* Southern Illinois University Press: Feffer & Simons, Inc.: London and Amsterdam, 1954, 1967.

Chapter 6

Antioch College

As an example of a utopian college, Antioch has a one hundred and fifty year history ranging from the height of utopian communities in the United States through wars, generational, and economic cycles to the present. It has changed, but still retains the idealogical tenets of its original founder and first president, Horace Mann. What has made Antioch retain its basic utopian beliefs throughout the years? The following chapter follows the course of Antioch's history and shows where the generational patterns, resistance to the dominant American culture, espousal of feminist educational beliefs, and cooperation with open-minded thinkers, be they philosophers or business people, have insured its continuation and academic originality.

Antioch University is perched in a small village on a plateau in southern Ohio between two actual, yet also symbolic, valleys: the one to the east contains Glen Helen, the 1,000-acre wooded preserve owned by Antioch, located to the west is Wright-Patterson Air Force Base with its government security, secret projects, and chain-link fences. Glen Helen symbolizes the Arcadian dream of the nineteenth century carried into the modern environmental consciousness. Wright-Patterson Air Force Base, which was one of the major centers during World War II and still is a military stronghold, has the modern technological emphasis of a military world. Antioch rises above these two disparate worlds, struggling to continue its strong ethical and moral history into the 21st century.

Antioch in Yellow Springs, Ohio is an island of intellectual and cultural broadmindedness, set in a middle American, mid-Western, and middle class environment. Antioch might be physically located in the middle of all this middle-mindedness, but it is one of the still centers in our materialistic, modern American hurricane. Antioch is a quiet eye of the storm. How did one of the oldest institutions of higher education in Ohio carry out a tradition of respecting and educating women and African-Americans from its beginnings in 1853 to the present day? What was the seed that made this university so different from the others in Ohio and from the more traditional and conservative mindset of southwestern Ohio?

The history of Antioch college parallels the birth of many other American nineteenth century colleges with their visionary dreams, ambitious building programs, and inevitable fights between opposing "carriers of the flame." Like many other colleges Antioch was founded by a religious order. In this case, the religious body was a then new group, the Christian Connexion, which arose in the eastern United States in the early nineteenth century and was said to differ from the Unitarians only in that it had a better name.

> A real difference existed, however, in the Christian's advocacy of vigorous proselytism through revivals and prayer meetings of an emotional nature. The Christians, despite their professed liberalism, were at times bigoted and narrow and were for many decades distrustful of education, even for the ministry. But the prospects before a vast, expanding country with a rapidly increasing population, gradually convinced the Christians that their duty lay in promoting education among themselves.[1]

As with most ideas, the concept of founding a college was not new, especially by a religious group which wanted a place to promote and educate its followers. Instrumental in pushing this realization ahead was the founding of the Meadville Theological School in Meadville, Ohio by the Unitarians in 1844. Not to be outdone by the Unitarians, the Christian Connexion, lead by Simon Clough, a Christian minister in New York City, urged their denomination to establish both a university and a Biblical school.

Although the Christians were distrustful of education, their competitive and egotistical drive to found their own college made them open to the supposedly practical ideas of Alpheus Marshall Merrifield, a building contractor of Worcester, Massachusetts. He visited the Christians in New England and New York in 1849–1850 promoting the importance of founding a first-class college. Armed with a practical knowledge of building and with a strong political sense, he was instrumental in the physical origins of Antioch College.

On May 8 and 9, 1850, an informally chosen committee on education, including Merrifield, formulated the plan for Antioch College which was presented and approved by a meeting of delegates from Christian congregations in the United States and Canada held at Marion, New

York on October 2, 1850. The committee resolved that equal educational privileges should be extended to both sexes, making Antioch the second coed college in the United States and the first with all educational privileges of an equal nature. Most of the delegates to the Marion convention were doubtless in favor of a denominational college, since at that time, nearly all colleges were denominational. But instead Antioch became non-sectarian through the influence of the more liberal leaders, many of whom later became Unitarian ministers. The educational seed of ideological openness was put forth, now the reality had to manifest.

Merrifield was the builder of the dream. He was the first treasurer of the college and one of the heaviest contributors to the new institution, giving it $1,000. He was on the two committees that chose the location and site and which secured plans and costs for the college buildings. The committee on drafts and estimates recommended the construction of three buildings—a main building and "male" and "female" dormitories. The two dormitories put into reality the revolutionary concept, at that time, of equal education for women.

Merrifield presented plans for the three buildings which were approved. After looking at eight other communities in Ohio, the state which was chosen for the college because of its Christian Connexion financial support, the sub-committee selected the site for Antioch Hall in a stump-filled wheat field in Yellow Springs, Ohio. Not using a bookkeeper and going over the original estimate of $50,000 to a final price of $120,000, Merrifield built the original buildings using himself as the building agent. Antioch Hall was at that time one of the largest buildings west of the Alleghenies.

The greatest ethical and ideological coup of the upstart college was the selection of Horace Mann as its first president. Eli Fay, of the Committee of the Faculty, approached Horace Mann for the presidency with the promise that the new college would be both co-educational and non-sectarian, which persuaded Mann to accept the offer.

Horace Mann had left his educational and legal work in 1848 to succeed John Quincy Adams as a member of Congress. Tiring of politics and missing his family, he vowed to return to academe. Many thought that it was strange that Mann would even consider accepting the Antioch offer, because he was at the height of his career. He had world-wide fame as an educator, and his published works were known in most European countries. For his rehabilitation of the common schools of Massachusetts he had received the honorary degree of Doctor of Law from Harvard (1849) and from his alma mater, Brown.

This leading American educator was promised a free hand in the development of the co-educational college in the then-remote West plus a promised relief from financial worries. At fifty-six Horace Mann left many friends, family members, and a cultural life to move to Yellow Springs to develop his own view of an ideal college.

Upon the base of non-sectarian and co-educational learning, Mann added the premise that the moral tone should be of the highest and that no diploma would be granted to any student whose character was in the least bit questionable. He was against any grading system and the competitive awarding of prizes, because he felt that competition should take the form of self-improvement and furthering one's own education. He also sought to stamp out bad health habits, since he believed mental and moral health depended on the physical body's health. He was non-racist and stood firm when the president of the Board of Trustees, Judge Aaron Harlen, resigned in protest at the admission of the first African-American.

How did this moral New Englander, who modeled the curriculum of Antioch after that of Harvard, fare in his creation of the "little Harvard of the West?" Unfortunately, Horace Mann encountered many of the problems of transforming dreams into reality. The school was bankrupt, which was not his fault, by 1857, and the men who brought it to that state then blamed him. Religious wars flared up between the faculty, townspeople, and the trustees. These different groups distrusted Mann, because of his liberal views, causing him to exclaim that he was living "among people with souls so small that a million sprinkled on a diamond would not make it dusty!"[2]

Horace Mann was a just and great leader as the first president of Antioch. He worked long hours, often without pay, while supporting his family as a lecturer. He loaned money to the college and deserving students who cheered him when he returned from lecture tours.

The college was insolvent the day it opened with the scholarship money and endowment already spent on the buildings. The lack of reality with which the Christian originators operated was shown by their projected plan to run a first-class college with an enrollment of 300 and a faculty of nine on an annual income of $6,000. The college was in debt by $75,000. in 1855, and the debt continued to grow, because of the excessive interest rate of 12% then allowable in Ohio.

Mann and several of the trustees pledged everything they owned to the college. The college went bankrupt and was sold at a public auction in 1859, luckily to a friend of the college, Francis Palmer of New

York City. A new board of trustees and new charter prohibiting debt were then installed.

Mann had tried to resign in 1856 and 1857, and then the task of the reorganization of the college had fallen on his increasingly frail shoulders. He had always been in delicate health. But he took on the administrative responsibilities, plus doing much of the teaching himself, since some of the instructors accepted positions elsewhere. He was so exhausted that he was often unable to eat or sleep.

At his last commencement speech in 1859, he said: "I beseech you to treasure up in your heart these my parting words: Be ashamed to die until you have won some victory for humanity."[3] Weak, worn-down, and burning with fever, he died on August 2, 1859. On his deathbed, he met with each of the students remaining at the college for the summer, encouraging them, and even absolving a note of money he had loaned to one of them.

Horace Mann had died for his dream, but his vision remained for years with the financially struggling college. A later Antioch president, Algo Henderson, connected Mann's reign at Antioch with utopian thinking, as is shown in the following excerpt:

> In 1853, somewhat belatedly in the search for *utopia* [italics mine], Horace Mann came out to Yellow Springs, Ohio, as the first president of Antioch College. Antioch, of course, was not strictly a utopia—Mann was too hard-headed for that—yet it was one of the most progressive colleges of its day. Although Mann and his friends called it "the little Harvard of the West," it was in some areas far ahead of Harvard. It admitted students without discrimination as to sex, creed, or color; put women faculty on a par with men; emphasized the physical health of its students; stressed the importance of character as well as of academic proficiency; minimized the importance of grades (Mann called them "emulation" as an incentive to study); and even provided a few elective courses.[4]

Some of the traits that separate utopian colleges from mainstream colleges can be found in the early years at Antioch. Of course, many of these ideas are now part of the American public education system. Some are still to be found only in utopian colleges, which are often far ahead of the present Harvard in liberal open-mindedness. For instance, most colleges admit students of different sexes, creeds, and colors, but there are at present many exclusionary social apparatuses, such as fraternities, sororities, and eating clubs which stratify and separate the undergraduate college student body at many traditional colleges.

"Putting women faculty on par with men" varies from college to college and is a case where the larger culture dictates the behavior to a large degree. Equal pay, equal numbers of women to men faculty, and equal leadership roles are still to be gained at many colleges, even utopian ones.

The emphasis on physical health is an obsession in our society today. But Big Ten football does not necessarily contribute to physical well-being, and often leaves its participants crippled by mid-life. As Hutchins noted in his "university of utopia," extra curricular activities, but no football team, are encouraged. The sound mind in the sound body concept that Horace Mann endorsed seems to be a private commitment of contemporary students in utopian colleges rather than a college-wide policy, although health foods seem to predominate on the present-day utopian college campuses. Mental health is often attended to at an earlier stage, because of the living accommodations, small classes, and constant interchange between the faculty and students.

"The importance of character as well as academic proficiency" is a central idea in the ethos of utopian colleges. With an emphasis on community, environmental projects and concerns, and with attention to the individual, many of the students are different than their counterparts in the competitive grade-oriented schools. Not using grades as an incentive at these non-traditional colleges, students must tap their own creative sources and set on their own journeys of exploration.

A student of the Antioch of the eighteen fifties received an education similar to the best of the utopian colleges today. Those early students had a personal, one-to-one contact with the great minds of their day. They lived as equals, respecting each other without prejudice. They planned their own intellectual journeys and had the freedom to express their ideas in a safe environment. Horace Mann's legacy survives in spite of many people with "small souls" who have tried to extinguish the dream.

After over a half century of struggle with finances and almost out of business again, Antioch was revived and given a new direction in the nineteen twenties by a new president, Arthur E. Morgan. He was the chief engineer of the Miami Valley Conservancy which built several large dams and created green space after the Dayton Flood of 1913. He was elected to the post by the board of trustees, because he submitted a plan not merely for putting Antioch on its feet but again making it a pioneer in education.

Mr. Morgan was an unusual college president. An engineer and a man who had only six weeks of a freshman year in college, he had a practical educational philosophy. He felt that higher education trained people in narrow specialties or educated them in nothing at all. He designed a curriculum to give Antioch students a life purpose and philosophy, to make the quality of living finer, and to accelerate the process of social evolution. The Antioch, which he envisioned, would be different from the large universities training specialized technicians. Morgan's idea was to educate students to emphasize, either in business or the professions, their role as the entrepreneur or small proprietor.

The key to his vision was the work-study plan which had an earlier experimentation in 1906 at the University of Cincinnati's engineering school. Morgan's plan was for all students to acquaint themselves with the economic world which would test their ideas and develop strengths for creation of future small businesses of their own and would cut the cost of their education in half, enabling a greater diversity of students.

When Arthur Morgan took over Antioch, it had only 37 students and bankruptcy was only a few weeks away. When he drove out to see Antioch, which he had only heard about, he saw a shell of a college. What he also saw was the possible fruition of a long-standing dream to put his own educational designs for a college into reality. He said to his wife, Lucy, who was riding in the car with him, "It looks dead enough to do anything I want with."[5]

Here was Morgan's chance to get beyond what he thought was the limiting world of civil engineering, despite having achieved national renown in the field. In Burton Clark's words, "His commitments to engineering and to social planning were fathered by his image of a more perfect world. He moved from engineering to social engineering in pursuit of utopia, and his utopianism was a critical element in the revision of the college."[6]

As will be seen again and again, a charismatic leader with a utopian vision instilled life into an almost moribund institution. A somnolent, failing, Midwestern college became, in half a decade, a world-famous institution of good size, extraordinary vitality, and remarkable educational leadership. The co-op program, the stress on a serious life purpose, strong academics, the emphasis on small industry and community, and the promotion of democratic decision making were but a few of Antioch's distinctions.

One of the interesting parallels between Horace Mann and Arthur Morgan was their attraction to utopian thinking. Mann was in the inner circle of the Transcendentalists of Concord, and Emerson even commented on Mann's years at Antioch as being "what seems the fatal waste of labor and life at Antioch."[7] Mann was friends with the people surrounding Brook Farm and associated with Nathaniel Hawthorne, Bronson Alcott, Emerson, and Thoreau.

Arthur Morgan, who is characterized in current Antioch literature as being a "utopian pragmatist," was a scholar of the utopian Boston author, Edward Bellamy. Morgan even wrote his own study of utopias, *Nowhere Was Somewhere*. He believed in creating "pilot plants" or trying out ideas in smaller laboratory models. Just as he had constructed models for the building of the Miami Valley Conservancy District and the Tennessee Valley Authority, he planned to use Antioch College as a pilot plant which would feed ideas and experiments to the larger educational establishment.

But Morgan had not just attended to the visionary and academic aspects of the colleges, he had solicited business wealth. Charles F. Kettering was one of the strongest supporters of Antioch and had many similarities to Morgan. He was an engineer, an original thinker, outspoken, and most important for Antioch a supporter of innovative education. Kettering also had been a partner in the progressive Moraine Park School, a private secondary school in Dayton, Ohio.

Kettering is now remembered as the joint founder of the Sloan-Kettering Institute in New York and many automotive inventions including the self-starter. Kettering had followed the work-study programs at the University of Cincinnati and had hired many of the graduates. His following endorsement of the work-study program uses an engineering analogy:

> What gives cooperative education its strength is that it lap-welds theory from the classroom with practice on the job. It creates a weld that is much stronger than the butt-welding of a college degree followed by employment, the two touching at one line of contact.[8]

Kettering gave a science building and the library to Antioch plus supporting it in many other ways. One of the most interesting projects that he supported in the twenties is as contemporary today as when he envisioned it: he was concerned with the petroleum crisis which led him to consider the possibilities of converting organic materials into automotive fuels. His financial and ideological support of Antioch illustrates one of the successful combinations of visionary college presidencies with trustees who have a similar point of view.

Even after Arthur Morgan left the presidency of Antioch, he was an influence in both the town it was located and at the college. He returned to Yellow Springs, after building the TVA project, and became a fixture in the town. Morgan held the philosophy of small business as the answer to mindless industrial growth and sold his ideas to many a businessman in the name of idealism as well as profit. None of this was too remote from the Antioch program itself which contrasted the value of an education at a small utopian college compared to the education which was being offered by the traditional universities which added buildings and football teams rather than quality controls.

Life at Antioch continued with experimental education, even into the conservative fifties when: "Antioch had its problems, serious problems, but it proved to many of its students that they could work for their own individuality and also for a place in the world much as earlier generations of Antioch students had done under less permissive conditions."[9]

In 1957, Antioch used the concept of international education for undergraduates when its first group of students sailed for Europe to inaugurate the Antioch Education Abroad program in Besançon, France. This program was a major extension of Antioch education outside the classroom from its United States-based work-study program into the larger world.

In 1961 Antioch joined eleven other liberal arts colleges in Ohio, Indiana, and Michigan to form the Great Lakes Colleges Association to promote cooperation in strengthening each institution's educational program. In that same year Dr. George Stern of Syracuse found Reed, Antioch, and Oberlin heading a list of 67 colleges he studied and rated for high intellectual climate.[10]

Only thirty years after Antioch's work-study programs began, in 1964 a number of studies showed Antioch as one of the top ten colleges in the country in the production of young scholars and scientists. Antioch was one of only eight institutions in the United States with highest scholastic indices in all three areas of the sciences, social sciences, and humanities. Achievement scores of Antioch graduates in Area Tests of the Graduate Record Examinations placed them among the top five of all colleges using the GRE tests.[11]

James P. Dixon was president of Antioch from 1959 to 1975, and under his administration Antioch expanded from its Yellow Spring campus with a national and international work-study program to one with field centers. Antioch acquired the Putney Graduate School of Teacher Education at Putney, Vermont and established a Master of Arts in teaching degree program. The Antioch-Putney Graduate School of Education began operating in 1964 in Putney and in Yellow Springs.

In 1967 a center of the Graduate School of Education opened in Philadelphia. In 1970 a program to increase cultural pluralism began on the Yellow Springs campus, and an undergraduate center was opened in Philadelphia. In 1971, the San Francisco field center opened, and it evolved into Antioch West with centers opening in Los Angeles (1972), Seattle (1975), and other locations on the West Coast. In 1972 the Antioch School of Law in Washington was established with a clinical curriculum of work-study for J.D. students. In 1971, the trustees formally recognized Antioch to be a "complex institution of higher education with major units in addition to the Yellow Springs campus." In the 1970's Antioch developed from a liberal arts college with a network of educational units to a formal recognition as a university in 1978.

The most disruptive single event of the Dixon administration was the six week strike (or more properly, "lock-out') in the spring of 1973. The lock-out at Antioch was one of the later student strikes in the United States and had a follow-the-leader character instead of being a landmark event. The college declined in financial resources and numbers of students and faculty for more than a decade later.

Through national trends and student population shifts, Antioch expanded and contracted like a balloon. The field centers, which brought the Antioch concept to the whole United States in the 1960's and 1970's, were difficult to govern and maintain from the home base. Antioch gained stature and financial gain from its many field centers, yet when the law school and several other centers collapsed, they could have brought the whole system down with them.

Alan Guskin, the Antioch president who took over in 1985, told me: "It took twenty years to destroy Antioch, and we rebuilt it in seven years."[12] In *Insider's Guide to the Colleges*, Antioch is evaluated and includes the following comment: "The president, Alan Guskin, is popular and makes a genuine effort to communicate with the students."[13]

Alan E. Guskin gave a reflective State of the College Address on September 11, 1989 which was reprinted in *The Antiochian* which harks back to the idealism of the sixties. He wrote:

> To act on one's belief's, to seek change was the center—is at the center—of college life. But, probably at no college or university were such values taken to such extremes in the 1960's. . . .
> Student choice being the primary determination of an individual's education was debated furiously, throughout the country: Antioch's long term phi-

losophy of focusing on the student and student direct involvement in governance led to experiments with total emphasis on student choice.[14]

He goes on to discuss the difficulty with students and faculty geographically distant from Yellow Springs. The adult learning centers, which were supposed to create revenue, instead turned into an enormous drain on the creativity and resources of Antioch, as did some of the programs for serving minorities. Guskin observed:

> In effect, while Antioch suffered from severe financial problems in the 1970's and early 1980's, the core problem was the breakdown of The College which began in the late 1960's: that is the norms for behavior and the values that are accepted as directing community members' daily lives. The financial problems were symbols of a breakdown in the culture of the institution; the will and capability of people to act in ways that could maintain the health of the institution.[15]

Guskin reflects on the irony that Antioch, which had long espoused the ideals of the sixties, had moved beyond them to the point where "Antioch's values led it to more extreme activities and actions which too often pushed it to the edge and sometimes over the edge."[16] He felt that " Antioch took the values and commitments of the 1960's to heart and did not have enough of the natural cynicism and healthy resistance of other institutions to limit its excesses."[17]

The period of the sixties and its aftermath at Antioch points out a vulnerable aspect to colleges built on utopian ideals. Since they have already addressed so many of the evils of our society, they sometimes move into radically destructive behavior which threatens the institution itself. A middle road is necessary, in which idealistic concerns are balanced with practical considerations of governance and education. Goddard and Sarah Lawrence also faced these decisions in the sixties and seventies.

As president of Antioch, Guskin did not want to lose focus on some of the good qualities of the sixties which range from social justice to placing students at the center of their learning experience. He felt that often in the sixties, people "lost a sense of humanity, sense of civility and sense of humility about what can and cannot be done."[18] He hoped that the leaders of the present will carry on the positive spirit of the sixties with humility, forgiveness, civility, and mutual respect and trust.

Present-day Antioch is a university which consists of:

1. Antioch College in Yellow Springs, Ohio
2. Antioch New England Graduate School in Keene, New Hampshire
3. Antioch Southern California (Los Angeles and Santa Barbara)
4. Antioch Seattle in Seattle, Washington

From its student explosion in the 1960's and 1970's, in 1990 Antioch served approximately 3,000 students with only 591 at Antioch College in Yellow Springs. The Antioch dream is still alive and is stated in its brochure:

> Antioch students are expected to be active in and responsible for their own education, and then to be active and responsible as leaders in the institutions and communities in which they live and work. Antioch students of all ages are encouraged to become life-long, self-directed learners, taking charge of their own lives. Faculty are expected to remain active contributors to the intellectual dialogue of their professions while maintaining a primary emphasis on teaching and advising. Both students and faculty are expected to be active members of the community on their campus and develop a civic intelligence essential for a vital democratic society.
>
> Antioch remains committed to building on its long-standing heritage of making learning meaningful and vital and promoting social justice. For many generations, students have been encouraged not only to examine their values but to act on them.[19]

Antioch University today is still fighting the economic realities and "small minds" of Horace Mann's day, but it also has the important and still unique commitments of "making learning meaningful and vital and promoting social justice." Antioch is still physically located in what is described by the editor of *Ohio Magazine* as "Yellow Springs is somewhere else—beyond ordinary, this side of Utopia."[20] The grandparent of the other American utopian colleges, Antioch still educates from its Arcadian "this side of Utopia" base in Yellow Springs to carry on the progressive and experimental ideas from its over one hundred and fifty year old history.

Antioch is the historical guidepost against which the other utopian colleges are measured. Sarah Lawrence came into fruition while Antioch was being reinvented in the twenties. Antioch helped create The Union Institute. Goddard cooperated and worked with Antioch.

But the "downside" of Antioch must also be faced. Arthur Morgan is remembered as being dictatorial by present day Antioch people and other progressive leaders. James Dixon almost destroyed the college.

Antioch was not as "open-minded" or "utopian" as it might have been during the student strikes. Sometimes sexist and racist attitudes appeared, and sometimes a hierarchical structure was institutionalized. Often the words and utopian thoughts of its leaders, faculty, and trustees do not relate to their actions or the reality of daily life. These human failings sometimes keep Antioch from being as ideal as it might be in the same ways that befell some of the utopian communities.

Notes

1   Straker, Robert Lincoln, *Horace Mann and Others: Chapters from the History of Antioch College*, The Antioch Press: Yellow Springs, Ohio, 1963.

2   Ibid, p. 38.

3   Ibid, p. 42.

4   Henderson, Algo and Hall, Dorothy, *Antioch College: Its Design for Liberal Education.* Harper & Brother Publishers: New York, 1946, p. 1.

5   Hotaling, Dan, "Shangri-la Revisited or the Rocky Horace and Arthur Show," unpublished faculty lecture, May 30, 1986.

6   Ibid, p. 10.

7   Ibid, p. 7.

8   Leslie, Stewart W., *Boss Kettering: Wizard of General Motors.* Columbia University Press: New York, 1983, p. 286.

9   Filler, Louis, "Antioch Past, Antioch Present: Some Notes on its Continuity and Prospects," speech given by this Antioch Distinguished Professor of American Culture and Society, November 18, 1977.

10   Oldt, Esther, "Antioch College as an Experimental Institution," June 1, 1964. An unpublished paper written by Esther Oldt, a research associate in the Antioch Education Abroad Program.

11   Ibid, p. 2.

12   Interview, Sept. 22, 1990.

13   The staff of *The Yale Daily News*, ed., *The Insider's Guide to the Colleges, 1990*, St. Martins Press: New York, 1990.

14   Guskin, Alan E., "State of the College Address," *The Antiochian*, Spring, 1990, p. 11.

15   Ibid, p. 12.

16   Ibid, p. 12.

17   Ibid, p. 12.

18   Ibid, p. 12.

19   *Antioch College Brochure, 1989–1990*, p. 227.

20   Ibid, p. 227.

Bibliography

1. *Antioch College Catalog, 1989–1990*, Yellow Springs, Ohio.

2. Cremin, Lawrence A., editor. *The Republic and the School: Horace Mann on the Education of Free Men*, Teachers College, Columbia University: New York, 1957.

3. Dawson, J.D., Vice President and Dean of Students, Antioch College. "Changes in Antioch Over the Last 43 Years," April 19, 1967, unpublished article.

4. Downs, Robert B., *Horace Mann: Champion of Public Schools*, Twayne Publishers: New York, 1974.

5. Filler, Louis, "Antioch Past, Antioch Present: Some Notes on its Continuity and Prospects," Nov. 18, 1977, unpublished article.

6. Filler, Louis, editor, *Horace Mann on the Crisis in Education,*, The Antioch Press: Yellow Springs, OH, 1965.

7. Foster, Lawrence, *Antioch—The Unfinished Revolution*, "Bibliograph Essay," unpublished.

8. Interview with Alan Guskin on Sept. 22, 1990.

9. Guskin, Alan E., "State of the College Address, Sept. 11, 1989," *The Antiochian: Alumni Magazine*, vol. 60, no. 1, Yellow Springs, OH, Spring, 1990.

10. Henderson, Algo D. and Hall, Dorothy. *Antioch College: Its Design for Liberal Education*. Harper & Brothers Publishers: New York, 1946.

11. Hotaling, Dan. "Shangri-la Revisited of the Rocky Horace and Arthur Show," Annual Faculty Lecture, May 30, 1986, unpublished.

12. *Important Dates in Antioch's History*, unpublished 55 page paper.

13. Leslie, Stewart W., *Boss Kettering: Wizard of General Motors*. Columbia University Press: New York, 1983.

14. Mann, Horace, *Lectures on Education*, Arno Press & The New York Times: New York, 1969.

15. Messerli, Jonathan, *Horace Mann: A Biography*, Alfred A. Knopf: New York, 1972.

16. *Noteworthy Alumni of Antioch College: An Abridged Listing*, Antioch publication.

17. Oldt, Esther A., "Antioch College as an Experimental Institution," June 1, 1964, unpublished 20 page article.

18.   Spock, Judith Wood, Interviews, Summer, 1990.

19.   Straker, Robert, "A Brief Sketch of Antioch College: 1853–1921," unpublished 20 page article.

20.   Straker, Robert L., "Horace Mann and Antioch," *Antioch College Bulletin*, vol. XXXIII, no. 13, Yellow Springs, OH, July, 1937.

21.   Straker, Robert Lincoln, *Horace Mann and Others: Chapters from the History of Antioch College*, The Antioch Press: Yellow Springs, OH, 1963. An informative collection of chapters on the early years of Antioch College. Straker was preparing a history of Antioch which he had not finished at his death, and these chapters are what remain of it.

22.   The Yale Daily News Staff, editors, *The Insider's Guide to the Colleges, 1990*, St. Martin's Press: New York.

Chapter 7

Sarah Lawrence College

Sarah Lawrence College has been progressive since its inception and carries on many of the beliefs of Antioch, such as ungraded classes, a faculty-invested governance system, and a non-sexist and non-racist philosophy. Sarah Lawrence is an example of the utopian college which sprang to life in the open 1920's.

Sarah Lawrence is a small liberal arts college originally for women, which has admitted men since 1968. It is located in Bronxville, New York, a suburb of New York City in Westchester County. Because of its proximity to the city, Sarah Lawrence has always attracted creative students and an exceptional faculty. The cosmopolitan atmosphere in a tree-covered suburb with Tudor buildings combines the two qualities of Sarah Lawrence: liberal, urban thinking in a comfortable, suburban setting. Sarah Lawrence has always been one of the most expensive colleges in the United States.

Sarah Lawrence was founded in 1926 as a women's college by William Van Duzer Lawrence to honor his wife, "an old-fashioned, progressive woman."[1] She had recently died and her husband conceived of the college as a memorial to her. Sarah Lawrence, the woman, was a progressive reformer who founded the YMCA in Canada and was the President of the New York Exchange for Women's Work which was where financially deprived women sold their handiwork. Mrs. Lawrence also co-developed Bethune-Cookman College, a co-ed institution for African-Americans in 1922.[2]

William and Sarah Lawrence lived in the large house, "Westlands," the present centerpiece of the campus, from 1916 when it was built until he dedicated it to the new college in 1926. William Lawrence also built the Hotel Gramatan and the Lawrence Hospital in Bronxville. When he made his family estate into a college campus, Lawrence included twelve acres, a gardener's cottage, and stables. He also accompanied the gift with $750,000. in securities which brought the total property value to $1,250,000. in 1926.[3]

After Mr. Lawrence made his gift of the college, he followed his wife in death in 1927. A close friend and associate of the Lawrences carried out the plans for the college which they had made together. This friend was Doctor Henry MacCracken who was the then president of Vassar College, a progressive educator who was sympathetic with John Dewey, and who participated in the activities of the Progressive Education Association established in 1919.[4]

The educational ideas which were instituted at Sarah Lawrence when it originated are still in effect. The new college had a flexible curriculum, interdepartmental relationships, and student-faculty conferences. There was an elimination of grades, and students chose their own courses.[5]

Today a close faculty-student relationship remains the cornerstone of a Sarah Lawrence education where the ratio of students to faculty is eight to one. An intensity of teaching results from this ratio. "The effect of this commitment of faculty time is more direct faculty participation and involvement with students in the educational process than at any other major undergraduate college in this country."[6] This high faculty-student ratio and intense one-to-one and seminar style of teaching is what also has caused the college to be so expensive.

Sarah Lawrence today has retained its creative, open energy among the students and faculty, an atmosphere which also can be seen at the other utopian colleges. There are no faculty clubs at any of these experimental colleges, and a visitor to their campuses sees faculty eating with students, having coffee breaks over projects with them, and walking around campus together. The faculty become friends and role models rather than distanced professors who speak to large classes in a lecture style. At Sarah Lawrence the intermingling between different types of students and faculty can be seen any day in the college coffee shop. The atmosphere is lively, and the cross-section of students does not break into separate racial groups as I observed at many large traditional institutions.

When Sarah Lawrence was first conceptualized as an experimental college for women different than Vassar's more traditional version, the founders were not alone in the 1920's educational scene. Sarah Lawrence, Bennington, and Scripps were chartered specifically for women as higher education progressive schools. In fact, most of the experimental colleges chartered after 1919 were founded for women. Labeling a school as an all female institution after 1920 seemed to legitimize it as an experiment in education.[7]

Previously there had been female seminaries which had grown into colleges such as Goddard College. The earliest female seminaries were founded by Emma Willard (1821), Catherine Beecher at Hartford (1828), and Mary Lyon in South Hadley, Massachusetts (1836). Prior to the Civil War only three state universities accepted women at the college level: The Universities of Iowa, Wisconsin, and Utah. The first official co-ed college was Oberlin, founded in 1833.[8]

The idea of founding several women's colleges during the twenties as experiments in education in order to legitimize them is an interesting concept. These colleges stressed the more creative or artistic abilities of their students. These are traits which were also endorsed by the culture for women. Woman in the twenties were encouraged to be versed in the refined aspects of life, so that they could be better wives and mothers. This was a tradition reaching back into the nineteenth century in both the culture and in women's colleges.

All of the utopian colleges which were studied have encouraged the right brain activities which are usually identified with women. Their art and creative writing programs have usually been stronger than their science or math departments. Their graduates have leaned towards creative or artistic fields rather than banking, the brokerage business, or as M.D.s, which are looked upon as traditionally male professions. This conclusion is based on my own reading of their alumnae magazines. These colleges have graduates in the fields of banking or medicine, but they seem to be the exception to the rule.

The humanities are strong at Sarah Lawrence, as well as the other utopian colleges, and individualized teaching is in force. Teaching assistants do not do the work of the professors. Even holders of the Pulitzer prize are available and are known by their students as human beings rather than by reputation as in the larger research institutions.

Esther Raushenbush, a former Dean and President of Sarah Lawrence, discussed the basic concepts of a Sarah Lawrence education in a talk to the NYC-Sarah Lawrence workshop for College Teachers and Administrators in 1947. She said that Sarah Lawrence has "more than almost any other college in the country . . . been free to think about education, to plan ways of educating young people, to put these plans into practice, and to remake them as our experiments preceded and guided us."[9] Mrs. Raushenbush perceived the unique quality of the Sarah Lawrence education with the faculty having the freedom to experiment. Many colleges espouse this freedom, but do not always let their faculty have their own way. In the learning laboratory which is Sarah Lawrence, the students and faculty drive each other into new dimensions through their creative interchanges.

Esther Raushenbush explains what freedom in teaching can accomplish.

> This is why we believe in the greatest possible amount of flexibility in teaching, both in subject matter and in the way of using subject matter; that is why we do not believe in a series of required courses or in a core curriculum; that is why we do not believe that all students should begin by studying Plato and whip through the great thinkers and end with Freud and Einstein.[10]

According to Mrs. Raushenbush, Sarah Lawrence was taking a different course than the other educational institutions of the 1940's. She was against the then widely discussed Harvard plan, since she did not believe in required courses or a core curriculum. She also did not see the need to "whip through" great books from Plato to Einstein, which put her at odds with the "great books" type of education.

If Sarah Lawrence did not have a core curriculum, required courses, or teach "great books" courses, what did they do? Using the don system borrowed from Oxford, every student had their own don/advisor whom they met with once a week. The don helped the student pick three courses a year which were in different fields. Within these three areas of interest, the student meets weekly with the faculty teaching the course. The individualized teaching is done in this "don" context. Sarah Lawrence is like Oxford, but exists as an independent college without the larger university structure. In many ways, New York City with its diverse cultural opportunities and educational institutions assumes the role of the larger university.

Former president Raushenbush explored in 1947 what is the basis of Sarah Lawrence teaching.

> The most important thing we have learned here about education is that our teaching exists for the students, not the students for our teaching; that the principal job while teaching a subject is to teach a student; that one doesn't teach a "class" one only teaches people; that the test of good teaching is that it should reach and have meaning for the students who are being taught. And I should say that it doesn't make the least bit of difference how you have to select and organize the precious knowledge you have to impart . . . it is useless unless it is or can be made important to the students you are teaching."[11]

In this statement Raushenbush tips the traditional college classroom upside down: her priority is the students, not the "class" or "precious knowledge." Here the knowledge is only important when it is understood by the student. The standard system is not applicable here. Students are not objects to be force fed knowledge by the professor who lectures at them, manipulates them, and grades them.

Sarah Lawrence and the other utopian colleges care about the students. The faculty and often the administration focus on the whole person attending to their personal life and how it effects their whole college experience. The students have a voice and are listened to, not just looked upon as numbers to fill classrooms for enrollment purposes or as popularity contests. The showman-lecturer type is replaced by the quieter, more reflective teacher who engages the students in a sympathetic, not adversarial, manner.

Harold Taylor, as the former president of Sarah Lawrence, wrote a piece for inclusion in this book. In his notes he reflects upon his role as philosopher-president, the utopian community of Sarah Lawrence in the fifties, the experimental curricula there during those years, and the role of faculty at Sarah Lawrence.

* * *

An Accidental President: Some Notes on Sarah Lawrence, prepared for Constance Cappel by Harold Taylor September 1, 1991

As a contributor to the material gathered by Constance Cappel, I felt that it might be useful to include the following comments about my experience at Sarah Lawrence in the earlier years (1950's) of it's founding. I had not known the college before my first visit to it in 1945 when I was teaching in the philosophy department of the University of Wisconsin. I was first approached by a pioneer member of the Sarah Lawrence faculty, Mrs. Helen Lynd, who came to Wisconsin to represent the faculty-trustee search committee for a new president. I told Mrs. Lynd that I did not wish to be a candidate, that I was a teacher, not an administrator. Mrs. Lynd and her faculty and colleagues assured me that the trustees and faculty were looking for a president whose background was that of scholar-teacher and quite possibly would combine teaching with his presidency.

That was the way it turned out. There was no orthodoxy or programmatic education cited, nor was there any suggestion that either I or the college would follow a pattern set by John Dewey, William

Heard Kilpatrick or any other figure of importance in the progressive era.

The central point of action for Sarah Lawrence was the individual faculty member teaching his/her own courses in cooperation with their colleagues, and there were as many styles of teaching as there were students and faculty members. Robert Fitzgerald wrote letters to his class on the themes in Greek poetry; his students wrote replies. Rolf Altschul invited his students to join him in working on his research projects in chemistry. An enormous degree of flexibility in planning and teaching a curriculum was possible, because the classes were small and the teachers were free to be serious about the students. This meant that the students were serious about their teachers and together they formed something approaching a Utopian community of concerned persons dedicated to the learning available in the college. They also formed a political and cultural community by reason of the freedom they enjoyed to plan their own intellectual and cultural lives. The cultural environment was enriched on an almost daily basis by the contributions from the faculty members and students of original works and productions in theater, music, dance, painting, sculpture and films.

When I first arrived at the college, the fact that we included dance and sculpture in equal status with philosophy and the rest of the humanities was looked on elsewhere as a form of educational madness. Yet year after year the impact of the dancers and their choreography and librettos was a serious part of the aesthetic education of the student body. The rest of the country has by now caught up with Bennington, which in the 1950's nurtured Martha Graham in her famous summer programs, and Sarah Lawrence, which combined music, theater and dance in new forms of opera and has shown the way to invent new curricula within the framework of experimental colleges.

I have thought of my own role in all this as one of building a community in a way similar to an orchestral conductor who builds an orchestra by choosing his/her musicians and composers according to certain standards of performance and concern and giving them a sense of freedom to enjoy the daily work they have been trained to do. I have tried to judge in advance the quality of the appointee's interest in the life of the college and the personal development of its students. In making this assessment I include an effort to judge the quality and scope of the appointee's intellectual equipment and after that, simply hope for the best.

* * *

Sarah Lawrence grew in national reputation as a liberal, sometimes radical, college for women from the 1920's to the 1950's. In the early fifties Joseph McCarthy labeled many institutions and individuals with charges of Communism and giving aid and comfort to the Soviet Union by treasonable activities. Sarah Lawrence was subjected to some of the sharpest attacks. The college responded by drafting a statement to their board of trustees "reaffirming freedom of discussion, of teaching, and of association with faculty members which became a nationally known document."[12]

Esther Raushenbush commented on the McCarthy attacks on Sarah Lawrence and other progressive colleges in the following statement:

> The assaults take many forms. Here I will speak of two of them, apparently distinct from each other, but actually prompted by the same hostility to the best goals education can have in our time: the assault on schools which charges them with being politically subversive and with harboring subversive teachers, books, and ideas; and the assault on educational methods and practices variously called Modern Education, Progressive Education, Child-Centered Education . . . ideas and practices that have in the past twenty years added new dimensions to the education of children and adolescents."[13]

The assaults made on progressive schools in the fifties are similar to the very ones leveled at similar institutions and even all of the humanities in the eighties. The right-wing attack on "politically correct" ideas at present is an example of the same style of thinking. George Will in *Newsweek* made an attack on "deconstructionism." He mocked, ridiculed, and attacked the concept that what he calls the "victimized class" would have any right to criticize the white male Western tradition.[14]

Even in 1957 Dean Raushenbush was able to differentiate Sarah Lawrence from other colleges and universities of its day. She wrote: "Sarah Lawrence was from the beginning a faculty-run college; that is, many of the administrative responsibilities that usually rest with the President or The Dean, in this institution are shared with the faculty."[15]

Most of the utopian colleges are faculty-run and when they become fractionalized or have too many outposts from the central core, they lose their strength. When the faculty, and even the students, are deeply involved with the college they struggle, but the institution remains healthy. When they go into a hierarchical mode and exclude faculty and students from decision-making, they often become like traditional colleges and lose their sense of community and that of an intensified learning environment.

Dean Raushenbush goes on to write about Sarah Lawrence when she was a Dean in the fifties, and I was a student there. This statement is a contrast to what is found in most traditional universities, then and now.

> Teachers here have always had a large voice in what they would teach; department chairman have little power, chairmanships are rotating, and any member of a department can be voted into chairmanship by his colleagues. During the years of my administration there was no faculty tenure, and there were no official hierarchies of power.[16]

"No official hierarchies of power." What a utopian idea! But it was true, and it worked. With the right people who have attained a level of consciousness to not abuse such a system, a faculty can govern itself in an ideal fashion that brings educational harmony to students and the entire college community. Without a constant warlike state between administration and faculty, faculty and students, the task of sharing ideas, governing, and education become a unified and positive endeavor.

In 1957 Dean Raushenbush wrote about her vision of a utopian college which she named "Erewhon College." Many of the characteristics were to be found at Sarah Lawrence. This utopian vision of hers of a two-year, low-cost Sarah Lawrence as part of a large university was later used to form a "satellite" college (New College) of Hofstra University. She even used the names of the Sarah Lawrence faculty circa 1957 which she changed slightly. For instance, Jane Cooper who was a writing faculty member at Sarah Lawrence in 1957, became "Miss Cowper would have assigned to her students especially interested in writing and poetry."[17]

In the updated introduction (1966) to his book, *On Education and Freedom,* Harold Taylor wrote about Sarah Lawrence College in the fifties when he was president.

> In 1953, when this book was first published, I was president of Sarah Lawrence College, doing work which gave me great pleasure and instruction. In one way or another, nearly everything that I was interested in was happening at the college. There was a stream of new work from the students and faculty every year in music, theater, dance, literature, and social thought. The intellectual and political life of the world flowed through New York and had its tributaries on the campus. The major political controversy of America in the

1950's or, I suppose, of any time, anywhere—the issue of intellectual freedom and its McCarthyite manifestation—had its own series of episodes, suc-
cessfully concluded, at Sarah Lawrence. (This was no pleasure, but it was
overwhelmingly instructive.) The liveliness of imagination, the gaiety and the
seriousness of the students, along with the educational ideas of the faculty, all
combined to produce a community life which had an invigorating effect on
practically everyone in it, including the trustees and the president.[18]

Harold Taylor describes the Sarah Lawrence College which I also
experienced as a student from 1955–1959. The year 1959 was also
Harold Taylor's last year at Sarah Lawrence. Doctor Taylor acted as
much as a philosopher-in-residence, as he did as college president. He
was a visiting lecturer in classes, and played tennis every weekend
with anyone who was his match whether it be a ranked player or a
student. He always had time for a chat with students or faculty and
knew every student by name. He was a charismatic leader and as such
held the students spellbound during his speeches.

But in his essay entitled "The College President," Taylor disagrees
reluctantly with Robert Hutchins who thought that "the proper president is a philosopher in action, by which he implied that the president
should keep his time and mind free to think up decisive things for the
faculty and other educators to do."[19] Taylor, who in my experience
was a "philosopher in action" as college president, wrote about the
realities of such a position. He thought that "The college presidents
will find that no matter how much abstract thinking they do, the educational ideas resulting from the process will only be as good or as
helpful in improving education as other people believe them to be,
and as other people feel impelled to carry them out."[20] He here raises
the political question of leadership. No matter how charismatic or
enlightened the leadership is, human nature or group dynamics can
either carry out the ideas or bury them in faculty or trustee meetings.

Harold Taylor stated his concept of where the ideas for a reform in
education originate.

I believe that most ideas for the reform of education come as mine did from
the experience of people who react against what seem to them to be defects
in their own education, and who advocate the virtues they have found there
as the beginning of a new system. The ideas are usually recollected and trans-
formed into theory or criticism after the education has been completed and
then they are presented as a program of reform.[21]

Taylor followed the teachings of William James, Alfred North Whitehead, and John Dewey in his writings. He felt that they understood

education in a humanistic way, since they were all "teachers, both in university classrooms and in their written work, they have shown a continuous concern for the students themselves and a depth of interest in eliciting from a pupil the best of which the pupil was capable."[22] Again his emphasis, as was Dean Raushenbush's, is on student-centered education with a strong teaching, not research, emphasis.

In an address on "Moral Leadership and Education," Harold Taylor in 1951 said that "Leadership of the world, if it is to be accomplished at all in the United States, can be accomplished only in moral terms."[23] He believes in teaching the ideal of freedom, and in espousing progressive ideas for education and reform. Taylor gives an insight into the possible lifestyle of a utopian college when he wrote:

> By living in a community of teachers and students where standards of honesty and humanity are revealed in the daily work of learning the liberal arts. The liberal art which is most worth teaching and most worth learning is the art of finding the truth and standing by it under pressure.[24]

The spirit of Sarah Lawrence, the founder, and of the years of Harold Taylor's presidency live on at Sarah Lawrence College. It has grown, changed, and expanded its vision, but still retains the atmosphere where "finding the truth and standing by it under pressure" exist. In 1962 Sarah Lawrence established the Center for Continuing Education which was the first full-scale undergraduate program in the country specially designed for returning women students. Sarah Lawrence has pioneered in the founding of several graduate programs: a Master's program in Human Genetics (1969), a Master's program in Women's History (1972), and a Master's program in Health Advocacy (1980), which have served as nationwide models.

Sarah Lawrence today is a respected, financially-stable college of around one thousand students which carries on its distinctive history of student-based education. The college still retains a system of teaching where there are no graduate assistants, instructors, or adjunct lecturers. As the catalogue reports: "There is no hierarchy of faculty ranking at Sarah Lawrence. Each teacher is simply and fully a teacher."[25] But Sarah Lawrence must guard against what happened to Antioch when it became too large and instituted a top-down structure. If Sarah Lawrence loses its "faculty-run" history, it might become another "seven sister college" or just another traditional small college. The uniqueness of its educational history should be preserved and not diluted in an effort towards financial stability. An economically viable institution does not necessarily have to be a traditional institution. Sarah Lawrence has survived the McCarthy attacks and the violent cultural upheavals of the sixties where not all faculty were free of racist thinking. The utopian aspects of its history and philosophy should be preserved.

Notes

1   *Sarah Lawrence College Catalogue*, 1988–1989. p. 6.

2   McDonough, Colleen. *The Founding of Sarah Lawrence College: A Case Study of the Contradictions in Progressive Education*. Master's Thesis in Women's Studies. Bronxville, NY: Sarah Lawrence College, 1968.

3   Ibid.

4   Ibid.

5   Ibid.

6   *Catalogue*, p. 6.

7   Ibid, p. 35.

8   Ibid, p. 540.

9   Raushenbush, Esther. "Behind the Educational Design of Sarah Lawrence College. A talk to the NYC-Sarah Lawrence Workshop for College Teachers and Administrators. June 16, 1947. *Occasional Papers on Education*. Sarah Lawrence College: Bronxville, NY, 1979. p. 11.

10   Ibid, p. 13.

11   Ibid, p. 13.

12   Raushenbush, Esther. "Is Education Worth Having?" A talk to a conference at the AAUW, Reading, Pennsylvania. Oct. 18, 1952. *Occasional Papers on Education*. Sarah Lawrence College: Bronxville, NY. 1979. p. 28.

13   Ibid, p. 31.

14   Will, George. "Literary Politics." Newsweek, April 22, 1991. p. 72.

15   Raushenbush, Esther. "On Faculty Morale." A paper delivered at the Danforth Campus Community Workshop at Sarah Lawrence College. July 22, 1957.

16   Ibid. p. 54.

17   Raushenbush, Esther. "Erewhon College: A Sketch for a Small and Economical Liberal Arts College." 1957. p. 49).

18   Taylor, Harold. *On Education and Freedom*. Southern Illinois University Press: Carbondale, IL, 1977. p. 5.

19   Harold Taylor. *On Education and Freedom*. "The College President." Southern Illinois University Press: Carbondale, IL, 1967. p. 58.

20   Ibid, p. 59.

21 Taylor, Harold. *On Education and Freedom*, "Philosophy and the Teacher." Southern Illinois University Press: Carbondale, IL, 1967. p. 145.

22 Ibid, p. 159.

23 Ibid, "Moral Leadership and Education," p. 95.

24 Ibid, p. 120.

25 Sarah Lawrence College Catalogue, 1988–89, p. 9.

Bibliography

1. Lynd, Helen Merrell. *Field Work in college education*. Sarah Lawrence College publications: no. 5. Columbia University Press: NY, 1945.

2. Lynd, Helen Merrell. *Possibilities*. Rev. Ed. With the collaboration of Staughton Lynd. Bronxville, NY: Friends of the Esther Raushenbush Library, Sarah Lawrence College, 1983.

3. Lynd, Helen Merrell, and Pares, Sir Bernard, and Dello Joio, Norman. *Teaching at Sarah Lawrence College*. Sarah Lawrence College: Bronxville, NY, [1947?]. (shelved in Archives)

4. Lynd, Helen Merrell. *Toward Discovery*. Sarah Lawrence College: Bronxville, NY, 1965.

5. MacCracken, Henry Nobel. *The Hickory Limb*. Charles Scribner's Sons: New York, 1950.

6. Mattfeld, Jacqueline A. *A Conversation Piece—The Several Futures of Sarah Lawrence College*. Sarah Lawrence College: Bronxville, NY, 1968.

7. McDonough, Colleen. *The Founding of Sarah Lawrence College: A Case Study of the Contradictions in Progressive Education*. Master's thesis in Women's Studies. Sarah Lawrence College: Bronxville, NY, 1978.

8. Munroe, Ruth L. *Teaching the Individual*. Sarah Lawrence College publications: no. 3. Columbia University Press: NY, 1942.

9. Murphy, Lois B. and Raushenbush, Esther, eds. *Achievement in the College Years*; a record of intellectual and personal growth. Harpers: NY, 1960.

10. Murphy, Lois B., and Ladd, Henry. *Emotional Factors in Learning*. Sarah Lawrence College publications: no. 4. Columbia University Press: NY, 1944.

11. Pekelis, Carla. *Memories 1907–1941*. [Unpublished manuscript, 1979].

12. Raushenbush, Esther. "Behind the Educational Design of Sarah Lawrence College." A talk to the NYC-Sarah Lawrence Workshop for College Teachers and Administrators. June 16, 1947.

13. Raushenbush, Esther. *Occasional Papers on Education*. Sarah Lawrence College: Bronxville, NY, 1979. p. 11.

14. Raushenbush, Esther. "Erewhon College: A Sketch for a Small and Economical Liberal Arts College." 1957.

15. Raushenbush, Esther. "Is Education Worth Having?" A talk to a conference at the AAUW, Reading, Pennsylvania. Oct. 18, 1952. *Occasional Papers on Education*. Sarah Lawrence College: Bronxville, NY, 1979.

16. Raushenbush, Esther. *Literature For Individual Education*. Sarah Lawrence College Publications: No. 1. Columbia University Press: NY, 1942

17. Raushenbush, Esther. *Occasional Papers on Education*. Sarah Lawrence College, Bronxville: NY, 1979 .

18. Raushenbush, Esther, ed. *Psychology for Individual Education*, by Lois Barclay Murphy and others. Sarah Lawrence College Publications: No. 2. Columbia University Press: NY, 1942.

19. Richter, Melissa Lewis, and Whipple, Jane Banks. *A Revolution in the Education of Women: Ten Years of Continuing Education at Sarah Lawrence College*. Foreword by Esther Raushenbuch. Sarah Lawrence College: Bronxville, NY, 1972.

20. *Sarah Lawrence College Catalogue*, 1988–1989.

21. Will, George. "Literary Politics." *Newsweek*, April 22, 1991.

22. Raushenbush, Esther. "On Faculty Morale." A paper delivered at the Danforth Campus Community Workshop at Sarah Lawrence College. July 22, 1957.

23. Taylor, Harold, ed. *Essays in Teaching*. Harper: NY, 1950.

24. Taylor, Harold. *On Education and Freedom*. Southern Illinois University Press: Carbondale, IL, 1977.

25. Taylor, Harold. *On Education and Freedom*. "The College President." Southern Illinois University Press: Carbondale, IL, 1967.

26. Taylor, Harold. *On Education and Freedom*, "Moral Leadership and Education," Southern Illinois University Press: Carbondale, IL, 1977.

27. Taylor, Harold. *On Education and Freedom*, "Philosophy and the Teacher." Southern Illinois University Press: Carbondale, IL, 1967.

28. Warren, Constance. *A New Design for Women's Education*. Frederick A. Stokes: NY, 1940.

Chapter 8

Goddard College

Goddard College is another arcadian/utopian dream-turned-college as was Antioch, which originated with its utopian roots from New England Transcendental thought. Not having the urban influence that Sarah Lawrence did, Goddard developed its progressive philosophy in a rural setting which gave it a strong sense of community. The history of Goddard shows some of the generational problems.

Goddard College is not a creation of the 1960's as most people think, but was organized in 1938, as the spiritual heir to Goddard Seminary, chartered in 1863. Goddard College is located in Plainfield, Vermont while the seminary was in nearby Barre, Vermont. The seminary was a private coeducational academy begun by Vermont Universalists. A Massachusetts Universalist, Thomas A. Goddard, contributed funds to build the seminary, and his widow's funds helped to transform what had been Green Mountain Central Institute into Goddard Seminary. The school prepared young men and women for college.

Goddard Seminary's educational program was based on Universalist principles such as recognizing the sacred worth of the individual and emphasizing the development of character as an educational aim. The seminary was one of the first academies to make the arts an intregal part of the curriculum and to train teachers as part of a liberal education. Goddard Seminary, like Antioch College, was from the beginning non-sectarian, was not church-controlled, and received no funds from the Universalist Church. The humane Universalist values did help to influence the educational institution which became Goddard College.[1]

Goddard Seminary thrived in the late 19th and early 20th centuries when its enrollments were healthy and its programs were respected.

But as the public high schools became more widespread in New England, many private academies and seminaries went into a decline. In 1929 Goddard Seminary closed its doors to men and became The Goddard School for Girls, emphasizing culture and refinement. After struggling in the Depression, Goddard changed again in 1935 to Goddard Seminary and Junior College with a new head, Royce S. Pitkin, a graduate of the Goddard class of 1919.

"Tim" Pitkin, as most people knew him, was the right person for the job of transforming Goddard from a seminary into a college. He had grown up in nearby Marshfield, Vermont on a farm, and as a farmer's son did not have the impractical view of bucolic life that lead astray many nineteenth century utopian community members and leaders. In fact, he learned much from his early life on the farm and could use his background to avoid much of the "town and gown" division to be found in many college communities.

But Tim Pitkin was not an uneducated country bumpkin. He graduated from the University of Vermont and was a school teacher, principal, and superintendent in Vermont before going to Columbia University for his Ph.D. At Columbia's Teachers' College he came under the influence of William Heard Kilpatrick, the ideas of John Dewey, and was impressed by Bishop Grundtuig's Scandinavian folk schools.

He felt that education was a key element in living and growing, as did his mentors. He believed that purposeful living was the avenue to learning with change as its motivating force. The concept of growth in character as well as in knowledge and in practical skills was as important to him as theoretical sophistication. This type of education was tied to community, society, and culture, as an agency for intelligent change.[2]

The attitude of Tim Pitkin towards government and decision-making was as follows:

> We didn't have a hierarchical form of government for decision-making. Generally, my policy was to let an issue come to its own resolution, rather than step in as the authority. No society can exist without controls, but in the long run, those controls are determined by what people will accept. The need is to create situations in which students exercise control over group behavior, allowing for individual freedom and responsibility. The issue is one of individual rights and collective needs, and learning how one fits in with the other.[3]

Here is a leader who applies what I view as a necessary ingredient to the concept of a utopian college when he advocates a non-hierarchical government which works from individual rights and collective needs. Pitkin further explains his relationship with the faculty as one where they had long discussions before arriving at a decision. He writes that: "I never saw Goddard as a one-man show. In fact, I hesitated to make certain moves without faculty support. I never thought of myself as a political person."[4] He believed in getting as many people as possible involved in developing a proposal or idea.

As Goddard developed, Pitkin noticed that the longtime faculty were more educationally radical than the newer faculty members who were chosen for their scholarly backgrounds. These newer faculty were more oriented toward conventional methods than toward being experimental or progressive. When they remained at Goddard, they became more supportive of the school's basic philosophy. He felt that faculty should leave, if they were working at cross purposes with the Goddard idea, since "Black Mountain College was broken by faculty dissension."[5]

When Pitkin took over the Goddard Seminary and Junior College, he was working with the plan that Hutchins outlined in his University of Utopia: two final years of high school combined with the first two years of college for a four year junior college. At Goddard Junior College in 1938, Pitkin arranged a conference chaired by William Heard Kilpatrick and attended by Goddard faculty, trustees, and guests, which would outline a new program for a new Goddard. The Kilpatrick conference produced a plan for an experimental college with learning by facing real life problems, learning by participation in policy making, and learning to help maintain and operate the college. The plan also created educational opportunities for adults.

Many of the utopian communities and communes have sought rural environments and a working farm for their living experiments. Goddard chose the same route when it moved from the city of Barre to the Greatwood Farms estate in Plainfield. The estate consisted of the Manor House with formal gardens which was attractive enough to be used in the eighties as a movie set as well as for educational purposes. The administrative office, dining room, and theater are located in a large hay barn which was renovated in 1946. The president's office is located in the silo of the former barn.

The 200-acre rural campus creates in the real world, Goddard College, as the realization of the arcadian dream. Although the newer buildings are shoddy and lack architectural solidity except for the library, the feeling of a country estate as a seat of learning is an overpowering first impression of Goddard. This bucolic setting led to some of the difficulties that Antioch also experienced in the sixties and seventies. Because of its isolation from a major urban area, many students were in non-residential programs and only visited the campus briefly, if at all. The plant was increasingly difficult to maintain and heat during the long Vermont winters, which was a fact not lost on Sarah Alcott long before at Fruitlands, which was also in New England.

But the new Goddard in its campus in Plainfield was part of important changes taking place in American higher education. As the Goddard College catalogue states:

> The Progressive Education Movement of the 1920's and 1930's had already spawned the new Antioch, Reed, Bennington, and Sarah Lawrence, and such important, influential, and—sad to say—vanished institutions as Black Mountain, the Experimental College at Wisconsin and New College at Columbia University's Teachers College.[6]

The new progressive colleges shared a common philosophical base which I identify as "utopian." Goddard borrowed some ideas from these other colleges, such as group teaching and individualized study from Sarah Lawrence, and a form of work study from Antioch. Commitment to needs of the community and state with a curriculum that emphasized issues and problems rather than traditional academic subjects became the trademark of Goddard.

The sense of community and a community government was one of the main tenets of Goddard College. Tim Pitkin drew on the Vermont town meeting for inspiration. In a small college where the students were all residential, this system can be effective. During the Pitkin years some of the faculty who endured the isolation of the long Vermont winters said that: "Meetings are our social life." As with many utopian communities the sense of community is indeed the social fabric with which the system works. The ability for all members of the group to be heard can be a strengthening force and bond within the utopian college, community, or commune.

During the first year of Goddard's new existence (1938), some Goddard students arranged a meeting at Columbia University in New York with students from Goddard, Bard, Bennington, and Sarah Lawrence. They hoped that this would be a way to obtain help in organizing the Goddard community. One of the students when she returned said: "Funny thing, Tim, these people from the other colleges didn't seem to know what kind of government they had."[7] Community government was always one of the strengths of Goddard College.

During the Pitkin years the progressive educational philosophy of Goddard had students design, with the help of faculty, their own curricula, and students participated fully in the governance of the college. The leadership of Pitkin was much like the utopian pragmatism of Arthur Morgan of Antioch. Both men believed in a creative and open minded educational environment without a hierarchical structure. They both knew how to operate in the world, so that they could keep their institutions financially afloat. Both believed in the individual freedom of their students and faculty. As leaders they used the "think tank" approach to education. Without prejudice they encouraged a community of individuals who shared.

In his 1961 commencement address Pitkin evaluated his twenty-five years at Goddard. He said that one of the developmental mistakes was in adding the last two years of college in 1941, which resulted in a six-year program. This problem was resolved when Goddard became a four-year college in 1947.

Pitkin discussed the community government and said: "On many occasions students and staff jointly confronted the problems of an experimental college trying to make its way in a highly conventional educational world."[8] At the beginning of each school year the only rule at Goddard would be no smoking, except in designated areas, which was certainly ahead of its time. All additional rules were then instituted through community government. Pitkin comments: "Ultimately, decisions were made by students, who greatly outnumbered the staff."[9] He reflected that community government provided a forum for expressing opinion, releasing hostility, and for the continuous chastening of administration and faculty, so that "maintaining and advancing democracy is no picnic."[10]

Goddard grew from an enrollment of 100 in the fifties to nearly 2,000 in 1974 through the non-residential adult degree programs (ADP) for the B.A. and several master's programs. Royce Pitkin retired in 1969 and was succeeded by Gerald Witherspoon who was president from 1969 to 1974.

Gerald Witherspoon reactivated the community meetings which had become used less because of the increased enrollment and the fading health of Tim Pitkin. During the turbulent late sixties and early seventies, Goddard was a magnet for students from other institutions and many counterculture groups who were seeking a freer academic environment. Goddard, as had Antioch and Sarah Lawrence, had already achieved the freedom for which students in other schools were fighting.

The town meetings under Gerald Witherspoon ran into a number of problems. The process was enormously time-consuming with the larger student body, and decision-making became an end in itself with little follow-through. Some issues were so complex that not all community members would have informed opinions. Participation declined, and "many persons read participatory democracy to mean one man, one vote, and were not satisfied with working for 'a sense of the meeting.'"[11]

Because of the atmosphere of the times, the community meetings became "areas for propaganda and power plays, the expression of anger, the presentation of 'non-negotiable demands,' rather than forums for analytical, reflective, and creative thought."[12] To make the participation of a larger student body more workable, Witherspoon instituted a hierarchical structure with councils, chains of commands leading to the president, and began calling the community meeting, "The Assembly." The Assembly would now petition the "Coordinating Council, to review decisions and, if appropriate, refer them back to specific councils with recommendations for specific revision."[13]

Goddard, like Antioch, had grown too large and too reflective of the culture to maintain its original form of government and lifestyle. Both institutions are similar to Brook Farm when the new generation or ownership imposes a different lifestyle on the community. The founding fathers, in this case Tim Pitkin and Arthur Morgan, turned the reins over to a new generation who moved from the smaller "think tank" model to a corporate model hierarchically implemented. Both institutions went through these chaotic years implementing a top-down structure which alienated their formerly participatory faculty.

A Third World program was instituted at Goddard in the late sixties and lasted three years. But the Adult Degree Program, (ADP) Experimental Education in Further Education for low-income adults, and the graduate programs which began in this period, and were all mainly non-residential, were successful. But problems arose which were campus-based, for instance, after a prolonged occupation of the president's office on campus and the theft of college records, Goddard officials took action against the students as they did at many colleges throughout the country. "As President Witherspoon put it, a college must be first and last a free marketplace of ideas, but when the idea arises in that marketplace that the marketplace should be shut down, someone has to say a firm and effective 'No.'"[14]

The idea of community governance cannot become anarchy, as even the utopian colleges found out in the sixties and seventies. The "marketplace of ideas" must remain open in order to continue. Rhetoric and political acts pushed the idea of academic freedom to the point where the institution itself was threatened.

This violent era on campuses also caused Goddard to employ a security force for their students when several women students were raped by outside "visitors." The dilemma for utopian colleges is when the negative forces in the outside culture permeate the utopian lifestyle of the institution forcing it to institute the very instruments of the prevalent culture which they had chosen to reject, such as a security force and court injunctions against students engaged in a "sit-in." These utopian colleges are the magnet for the agents of change in the outside culture and as such are faced with choosing peaceful change rather than a violent one. At both Goddard and Antioch the campus was used as a learning laboratory which experimented with new concepts and educational programs to the point where the college's economic and social limits were tested.

From 1976 until 1980 I had the opportunity to be part of the Goddard story. Beginning as a part-time undergraduate teacher in the residential B.A. program, I became a full-time core faculty of the non-residential Masters program. The non-residential Masters degree from Goddard was similar to the non-residential Ph.D. at The Union Institute. In the seventies many of the students went from the Antioch and Goddard M.A. program to the Union Ph.D.

The non-residential programs at Goddard had many of the characteristics of the Chautauqua program of the nineteenth century, but they went beyond the correspondence school limitations of that program. At Goddard, Antioch, and The Union Institute a core faculty is the link with the institution while adjuncts in the area of specialization do the educational work in the learner's academic field.

The 1989–90 Goddard College catalogue describes the years of the late seventies, as follows:

> The roller coaster of demographics and cultural change took Goddard from a high point in its institutional existence to a low point. The baby boomers finished college and there weren't nearly as many new students to replace them. The income from tuition, which had historically provided the bulk of Goddard's revenues, dropped sharply. And American society itself changed;

experimentation seemed to yield to rigidity. The changes were too great for the college to handle easily, and by 1980 Goddard was warned that it could lose its accreditation unless it were put on a sounder financial footing. Goddard faculty, staff, and students faced the situation with a characteristic determination to pull through.[15]

What the catalogue omitted was the leadership throughout these years. Richard Graham followed Gerry Witherspoon as president and what often happens at other colleges happened at Goddard: the leader and the institution did not fit. From a distinguished career as an administrator in the Peace Corps, Graham looked, as had many teachers and administrators before him, at Goddard as a place to enjoy a country life without many stresses.

Instead he met a fractionalized college in which individual program fiefdoms resisted any interference from the central office. A loose corporate structure had been institutionalized with the money-making non-residential programs resenting their support of the financially dependent Goddard campus. The non-residential programs had satellite offices throughout the country which often looked at Goddard as a credentialing device. Very little sense of community remained, and the warring factions between different programs was similar to the interdepartmental battles in large research universities. Graham often complained of "crisis management" between his cross-country skiing and attempts to lead the bucolic life for which Vermont is known.

Although the ADP and graduate programs were making money from large student enrollments, the residential college could not meet its expenses, attracted counterculture students with drug problems, and had a declining enrollment. The local bank in Montpelier held notes on the Northwood campus, and the compounded interest was mounting. Richard Graham chose to leave and return to Washington, D.C.

The new president was John Hall, a concerned alumnus who had been active in the support and recruitment for the college, since he had graduated in the 1940's. Pitkin mentioned him when he wrote: "John Hall was another veteran who came to Goddard. He became chairman of the work program and brought some order into its operation."[16] John Hall agitated to be a member of the board of trustees when he was a student, and the community voted to send Hall and another student to board meetings. But as Pitkin observes: "The Board didn't appoint them as members, but that wasn't necessary for they could say anything they liked."[17]

When John Hall took over the presidency of Goddard, he was looked upon by some of the older faculty as someone who knew and worked with Pitkin and would return the college to those "good old days." He did, but I do not think in the way the founder would have taken. The local bank under new direction began calling in many of their loans which caused several local businesses to fail. Goddard had always had a good relationship with the bank under Pitkin, and the bank had always been lenient with Goddard because it was the major employer in Plainfield. John Savage, the administrator at the bank at that time, did not hold similar views.

In a closed door decision only known by a few insider faculty members, John Hall and the board of trustees decided to sell the only two money-making programs to a nearby military institute, Norwich University. Not only were the non-residential ADP and graduate programs sold, the name of Goddard was also sold with them to be used for a period of several years. These programs moved under the auspices of Vermont College in Montpelier which had been acquired by Norwich University. Most of the non-residential Goddard faculty and some administrators in these programs moved with them. Many of these faculty lived in other parts of the country and were not concerned about the original Goddard College. As with the second generation in a business, the salaried employees have different priorities than the first generation. This classic business takeover was executed by a military man who sold the moneymaking part of the college leaving a weak residential Goddard College in Plainfield with low enrollment, closed buildings, and the threat to accreditation hanging over it.

What a change from the thoughts of Pitkin concerning military power when he wrote in 1948:

> After the Second World War, instead of using our resources to educate citizens in the skills of maintaining peace, America poured its wealth into creating another military machine. Disregarding the teachings of Jesus Christ and Gandhi, and the lessons of history, it put its faith in force and an exhibition of military power. Instead of helping people learn to understand other peoples and to live with them, we drafted young men into training for war under the direction of men who displayed little understanding of the consequences to mankind of another worldwide conflict.[18]

But the idea transcended the institution, and in 1996 on the Vermont College campus in Montpelier the enrollment of undergraduate and graduate students reached almost one thousand adult learners.

Norwich University remains ten miles away in Northfield, Vermont while the Vermont College campus retains the educational philosophy of John Dewey and progressive education. The days of division between Goddard College and Vermont College of Norwich University have passed with cooperating faculty, and Jackson Kyle now serving as a vice-president of Vermont College.

The original Goddard College in Plainfield in 1980 acquired a new president, Jack Linquist, who trimmed Goddard's budget, consolidated the remaining programs, scaled down the administration, and sold part of the campus. The threat to accreditation was removed, and the enrollment went from 116 students in 1981 to over 350 in 1988 with 125 on campus.

In 1990 a new president, Dr. Jackson Kytle, was selected after Jack Linquist announced that he would not seek another term. Dr. Kytle came from another utopian college, Antioch, which went through parallel growth and contraction problems as Goddard. As the former Antioch University Vice-President for Academic Planning and Provost of its School for Adult and Experimental Learning, Kytle had an excellent background to take over the continuation of the dream at Goddard. After he was president for several years, Goddard is conducting another presidential search in 1997.

In the eighties when the military and business were booming, many private colleges were struggling. Goddard was hit by mounting expenses, major reductions in federal financing, and the difficulty of raising money for a small, endangered college. Kytle faced a bare-bones budget at Goddard and said, "Goddard's problems are not unlike those at Antioch."[17]

Dr. Kytle understood the ethos of Goddard when he said:

> Goddard and Antioch share a philosophy of education that emphasizes individually planned education and learning, through hands-on experience. It's tremendously important that colleges like these be protected in a time when liberal and progressive ideas are so often under attack.[19]

Dr. Barbara A. Mossberg assumed the presidency of a healthier Goddard College of over five hundred students in August of 1997.

Notes

1   *Goddard College Catalogue,* 1989–1990. Plainfield, VT. p. 3.

2   Benson, Ann Giles and Adams, Frank. *To Know for Real: Royce S. Pitkin and Goddard College.* Adamant Press: Adamant, VT. 1987. p. 300.

3   Ibid, p. 40.

4   Ibid, p. 41.

5   Ibid, p. 41.

6   *Goddard College Catalogue,* 1989–1990. p. 10.

7   Benson, Ann Giles and Adams, Frank. *To Know f or Real: Royce S. Pitkin and Goddard College.* Adamant Press: Adamant, VT. 1987. p. 40.

8   Ibid, p. 197.

9   Ibid, p. 197.

10 Ibid, p. 197.

11 Hamlin, Will. *Goddard College: Retrospect and Prospect.* 1974 Report to NBASC, p. 31.

12 Ibid, p. 32.

13 Ibid, p. 33.

14 Ibid, p. 47.

15 *Goddard College Catalogue,* p. 11.

16 Benson, Ann Giles and Adams, Frank. *To Know f or Real: Royce S. Pitkin and Goddard College.* Adamant Press: Adamant, VT. 1987. p. 116.

17 Ibid, p. 117.

18 Press Release, Goddard College, June 10, 1990.

19 Ibid.

Bibliography

1. Benson, Ann Giles and Adams, Frank. *To Know for Real: Royce S. Pitkin and Goddard College.* Adamant Press: Adamant, Vermont, 1987.

2. Goddard College Catalogue, 1989–1990. Plainfield, VT.

3. Hamlin, Will. *Goddard College: Retrospect and Prospect.* 1974 Report to NBASC.

4. Press Release, Goddard College, June 10, 1990.

Chapter 9

The Union Institute

The Union Institute is built on the educational foundations of Goddard and Antioch and espouses the equal treatment of women stressed at Sarah Lawrence. As an experiment in higher education, its roots go back to the work-study of Antioch and the non-residential model of the Chautauqua movement.

The Union Institute, which was founded in 1964 and incorporated in 1969, is located in a large Tudor-style building which is a historical landmark in Cincinnati, Ohio. It was located in Yellow Springs, Ohio in the seventies and rented office space in a Cincinnati high-rise building in the eighties. The Union Institute moved to its newly acquired building in 1989. This year was an eventful one for the institution, because it also changed its name from the Union for Experimenting Colleges and Universities to The Union Institute on July 1, 1989. This institution is mainly non-residential, holding its colloquiums and seminars across the United States. The acquisition of a permanent building for its administrative offices was a major step for the originating university of UWW, the University Without Walls. After twenty-five years in existence The Union Institute moved within its own walls.

Union, as I shall refer to it for simplicity in this book, had its beginnings at Goddard College, although most people associate it with Antioch, because it was located in Yellow Springs. Royce Pitkin wanted to celebrate Goddard's twenty-fifth year in 1963 and invited representatives from many experimental colleges to the Vermont campus. In that winter the presidents and other executives of eight colleges came to Goddard to discuss the impact of the future of the experimental college in America.

At this time Pitkin was having difficulty with his own definition of "experimental college," since those colleges who came to the conference ranged from "Stephens, which had been doing some experimentation for years but of a more conservative sort, and Reed, where a new kind of college was started about 1912 and from which the leaders of Bennington and Sarah Lawrence had come."[1] The terms "progressive" and "experimental" have been used to describe all the colleges included in this study. These definitions sometimes become as difficult as "utopia" when applied to different institutions. Some places are more or less progressive, experimental, or utopian than others.

Royce Pitkin arrived at a definition for experimental colleges which is as all-encompassing as describing a utopian college as a "good place." His definition was as follows, and is so broad a definition as to describe most colleges:

> An experimental college is one which engages in experimentation. This experimentation can include a great variety of things. An educational experiment is a process in which an institution attempts to deal with a problem in education by formulating a hypothesis about the problems, cause and possible solution, then devises a means of testing the hypothesis and measuring the results.[2]

The present president of The Union Institute, Robert Conley, traced the historical roots of Union beyond the history of progressive education or experimental colleges when he said in an interview:

> We are rooted, simultaneously, in the nineteenth-century tradition of German universities with their emphasis on individual research; the Oxford and Cambridge tradition with their tutorial rather than broad-based format; and the American research universities of the 1950's. The individual learner is the center of all that we do. Therefore, our unique tradition avoids any structure that depersonalizes, or reduces the learner to a cipher.[3]

In 1963 at Goddard the college administrators felt isolated. They were not having as much contact with Bennington, Sarah Lawrence, and Bard, as they had earlier. During the 1963 conference of experimental colleges Woodburn Ross, director of Monteith College at Wayne State University, made a proposal for an organization of these colleges. They set up an organizing committee which consisted of James Dixon, president of Antioch, Paul Ward, president of Sarah Lawrence, and Royce Pitkin, President of Goddard.[4]

In 1964 the Union for Research and Experimentation in Higher Education was started by this committee. The Union was first seen as an organization that would work with member colleges "to support the interchange of ideas and the role of experimental colleges, and to help them have greater impact in America."[5] This group engaged Sam

Baskin, who was working at Antioch, as president of the Union on a part-time basis.

In 1965 the Union had its first annual conference in February at Goddard. The member colleges at that time included Antioch, Bard, Northeastern Illinois College, Loretto Heights, Monteith, Nasson, New College at Hofstra, Sarah Lawrence, Shimer, and Stephens. In ten years the membership grew to over thirty colleges.[6]

Royce Pitkin writes about these historical roots when he remembers:

> The union started the University Without Walls program, UWW, which was a clear copy of Goddard's Adult Degree Program. When the idea was presented to Goodwin Watson at Columbia, he said, "They've already done that at Goddard"—referring to ADP. Even the Union Graduate School Program is similar to ADP. As a matter of fact, Evelyn Bates, who had developed ADP, helped to formulate the UGS program as a Goddard representative on the committee that worked out the guidelines.[7]

The University Without Walls program which originated at Union and was used at many educational institutions had an influence on American education that is known internationally. Many colleges looked at education differently after their exposure to UWW, and incorporated it into their own educational systems.

In 1971 The State of Ohio authorized the Union to award both doctoral and baccalaureate degrees. In 1972 it was granted candidacy status, and in 1974 candidacy was extended to the doctoral level. In 1976 Union redefined its mission. It saw the institution as:

1. A consortium of developing programs and projects between and among member institutions and seeking to influence public policy in education.
2. A degree-granting institution providing learner-centered, individualized experiential, field-based education at the under-graduate and graduate levels.
3. Part of a movement, participating in national and international efforts to promote and facilitate the development and growth of alternative education.[8]

From 1976 to 1980 I was a graduate learner at Union at the same time I was working as a graduate core faculty at Goddard. These years were difficult and confusing ones at both institutions. The Union and Goddard were carrying a new form of non-residential education to eager adult learners who were unable to obtain such an education on the graduate level from a traditional institution. While the academic process was exciting and ground-breaking, the supporting institutions were going through difficult political and economic times. Organizational and financial problems caused the resignation of the president of Union and several senior administrators.

In 1978 UCEU or Union went into Chapter 11 bankruptcy, and the NCA recommended that candidacy status be terminated. The UCEU appealed the decision, and candidacy status was extended to the spring of 1981. UCEU again sought status at that time and was granted candidacy status until April of 1985. In February 1985 the Commission voted accreditation to the Union.[9]

Roy P. Fairfield, a core faculty member at Union and the administrator in charge of the Putney-Antioch graduate program in the 1970's, wrote a book, *Person-Centered Graduate Education*, which was published in 1977. In this book he discusses many of the strengths and difficulties of person-centered graduate education and writes extensively about the Union Graduate School. The many opposing thoughts at that time between different ideologies and groups appear in Fairchild's text. He traces the roots of the Union Ph.D. program to "many founding fathers," but Fairfield thought that it rests solidly on "the philosophical foundations laid by men like Jean Jacques Rousseau, Friedrich Froebel, John Dewey, and phenomenologists."[10]

Many requirements were changed in the Union Ph.D. program in the seventies, for instance the length of the colloquium from one month to the current ten days. When I attended in the seventies, a Ph.D. degree could be obtained in one year. I sat on two committees as a peer which were chaired by learners who completed in one year. One was a superintendent of a school system in Vermont and the other a family therapist in Philadelphia. Both programs were heavily documented, but the crossover between their professional and Ph.D. work was not always clear. The Ph.D. now requires two years minimum and takes three and a half years on an average to complete. I resigned from the Ph.D. program in 1980 because of the insecure financial and accreditation situation at that time and other priorities in my life, but reentered in 1987 and received a Ph. D. degree in 1991.

Today The Union Institute is thriving with both a highly respected Ph.D. program and an undergraduate division. The reaccreditation recommendation in 1989 was for The Union Institute to be accredited at the doctoral level until 1999. In the previously cited report of the accreditation team, they found that Union is financially and educationally stable with an institutional commitment to both interdisciplinary and socially significant concerns. They validated that Union has a low student attrition and is student centered. The accreditation team found an excellent selection process and orientation for both faculty and students with a focus on process. They also remarked on the strong disciplinary underpinnings which result in a sense of community.

The Union Institute with its graduate program, which is similar to those of Goddard and Antioch, utilizes the adult learner based, non-residential model that was an expansion of the Chautauqua program. The origins of Union are different than the other colleges, since it sprung fully conceptualized out of a committee of progressive educators with similar educational viewpoints. These educators also endorsed a non-competitive extension of their ideologies which would be available to their students on the Ph.D. level. The University Without Walls program took on a life of its own and became integrated into mainstream American higher education.

Because Union did not have a residential campus many of the conflicts which existed in residential utopian colleges and communities did not arise. The leadership issue was one of the few problems which remained. The leaders by committee plan which was used in the origin of Union was followed by a succession of leaders throughout the seventies. The ideology of the institution vacillated yearly, but usually was more radical than liberal.

When Robert Conley became president, he was the "utopian pragmatist" type of leader like Arthur Morgan of Antioch. The issues of accreditation and financial stability were addressed and solved in a more liberal than radical fashion. Like Sarah Lawrence, Union moved back towards the center of American education without changing its basic beliefs, because traditional education had incorporated many of its founding educational ideas and found them acceptable.

Union has a learner-centered education model for adults who would not be able to obtain their degrees in many traditional Ph.D. programs. The learners can work while they are enrolled in the program. They are older, experienced, and often in mid career. They could not relocate to attend a full-time traditional Ph.D. program with classes, grades, teaching assistant duties, and the many other peripheral activities which have lengthened the average Ph.D. program in the humanities to eleven years.

The Union Institute is the natural outgrowth of the other groundbreaking utopian colleges. All are non-sectarian, non-sexist, and non-racist. They encourage the individual pursuit of knowledge with flexible subject matter. As one of these utopian colleges or universities, Union is faculty-run, in most instances, and has no tenure. Although students are far-flung, a sense of community is developed through the colloquium, peer days, and networking by letters and via electronic communication exchanges, and over the telephone. The members of each Ph.D. committee often form a solid support group, because the committees are circular not hierarchical in structure. Original thinking and research is encouraged and not fed back into the system for the greater glory of the institution or for the use of publication-hungry mentors.

Elizabeth Minnich summed up the current status of community at Union when she compared it to women's communities and culture. She wrote:

> Today, an emphasis in women's communities on undoing rigid divisions be-tween gendered roles and the public and private also suggests kinship with the Institute's vision of education. We build into our programs concern for personal as well as intellectual growth, for political and social as well as aca-demic and professional analysis. As we in the Graduate School struggle to maintain *our* community so that we may work toward a kind of wholeness in learning and living, community among women also provides a safe place in which to create similarly difficult, visionary alternatives that are needed far beyond these communities.[11]

The Union Institute has created a "visionary alternative" in educa-tion which makes it one of the most financially and educationally suc-cessful utopian colleges in this study. This utopian institution has run counter to traditional American education. This difference is shown in a fund-raising letter from the president of The Union Institute, Robert T. Conley, when he refers to this institution as pursuing "even greater positive notoriety."[12] This "notoriety " was contained in the context of his following two paragraphs.

> Being part of The Union Institute family means constantly striving to gain acceptance for our educational innovations and new approaches to adult learn-ing. For several years, we have been demonstrating the academic quality of our programs. In November last year, our academic accreditation was very favorably renewed for ten years. Since, then the University has been identi-fied among the top institutions of higher education in the country.
> We continue to prove ourselves and support our alumni in the profes-sional world, in environments where some traditionalists still have difficulty associating educational innovation and diversity with quality. I am happy to

report that the University is making very encouraging progress in becoming an even better recognized leader in American higher education.[13]

The Union Institute has achieved financial viability, but some faculty members, who helped mold it in its inception, feel that it has lost some of its utopian concepts. They think that the move to a more traditional philosophy of education has weakened its uniqueness. Colin Greer has spoken out against the move to business institutes and the Adler-dominated forms of psychology. The dispersion of nationwide faculty weakens its influence on the Cincinnati-based administration. In its move to financial security, The Union Institute should watch that it does not lose its utopian direction by becoming hierarchical and corporate in structure and traditional in its educational direction.

Notes

1   Benson, Ann Giles and Adams, Frank. *To Know for Real: Royce S. Pitkin and Goddard College.* Adamant Press: Adamant, VT. 1987. p. 107.

2   Ibid, p. 208.

3   Conley, Robert. "President Conley on State of the Union." Interview. Network: Vol. 9. No. 1. Fall, 1989. p. 10.

4   Benson, Ann Giles and Adams, Frank. To Know f or Real: Royce S. Pitkin and Goddard College. Adamant Press: Adamant, VT. 1987. p. 108.

5   Ibid, p. 108.

6   Ibid, p. 209.

7   Ibid, p. 210.

8   Conley, Robert T. *Accreditation: Reports of the October 1989 North Central Association Team Visit and the Reaccredition Recommendation for The Union Institute.* Oct. 23–25, 1989. p. 11.

9   Ibid, p. 11–12.

10 Fairfield, Roy P. *Person-Centered Graduate Education.* Prometheus Books: Buffalo, NY. 1977. p. 16.

11 Minnich, Elizabeth. "On Some Meanings of Community and Culture for Women." *Network:* Volume 10, No. 1. Summer/Fall 1990. p. 24.

12 Conley, Robert T. Letter to Friends of The Union. January 29, 1991.

13 Ibid.

Bibliography

1. Benson, Ann Giles and Adams, Frank. *To Know for Real: Royce S. Pitkin and Goddard College.*Adamant Press: Adamant, VT. 1987.

2. Conley, Robert T. *Accreditation: Reports of the October 1989 North Central Association Team Visit and the Re accreditation Recommendation for The Union Institute.* Oct. 23–25, 1989.

3. Conley, Robert. "President Conley on State of the Union." Interview. *Network:* Vol. 9. No. 1. Fall, 1989.

4. Conley, Robert T. Letter to Friends of the Union. January 29, 1991.

5. Fairfield, Roy P. *Person-Centered Graduate Education.* Prometheus Books: Buffalo, NY, 1977.

6. Minnich, Elizabeth. "On Some Meanings of Community and Culture for Women." *Network:* Volume 10, No. 1. Summer/Fall 1990.

Chapter 10

World College West

World College West was founded on progressive tenets and was often described as experimental or progressive. Although it did not have close founding ties with the other four utopian colleges, it was the Western (American West) example of many of their basic philosophies and beliefs. Students, admissions counselors, and many educators viewed this college as one of the "utopian colleges."

World College West discontinued classes in the fall of 1992, after I had written the first draft of this book. The college closed with the final legal and financial details completed by its board of trustees. World College West was an exciting experiment which lasted longer than Brook Farm. Its demise appeared to hinge on the difficult transition from a first generation charismatic leader to a second generation.

World College West was the youngest of the five utopian colleges which were analyzed. Founded in 1973, the college became a fully-accredited, four year liberal arts college dedicated to world studies. It was the first college in America to require every student to study abroad through total immersion in the culture of a non-Western country. World Study programs were conducted in China, Mexico, Nepal, and the Soviet Union.

Barron's Guide to the Best, Most Popular and Most Exciting Colleges listed World College West as "One of the most exciting colleges in the United States."[1] In 1988 Kiplinger's *Changing Times* included the college as one of the 42 "high-quality, low-priced" colleges in the nation (and the only private college in California), selected by a panel of higher education experts.[2]

The founder of World College West, Richard Gray, was alive for both the founding and the demise of the college. In contrast, The Union Institute was conceived and founded by a group rather than an individual. A charismatic leader like Horace Mann of Antioch and

Harold Taylor of Sarah Lawrence, Richard Gray created a college which reflected his own dreams of education.

When Steve McNamara of the *Pacific Sun* wrote an article about World College West in 1981, he described Richard Gray as follows:

> It all seems so hopelessly idealistic. Young Philadelphia ad man is jolted by the death of his father, heads West with his understanding wife to enroll in a theological seminary, becomes a campus minister for eight years, gets his Ph.D. at Berkeley and decides to create a completely different four-year college of his own, one to nurture leaders toward a humanistic world view.
>
> This is a fantasy—not practical in any way—isn't it? "I agree. It makes no sense at all," says Richard Gray, president of World College West and the man who has lived the dream.[3]

Here are the descriptions that often arise when describing a utopian college: "a completely different college," "a humanistic world view," "a fantasy," and "a dream." Richard Gray also embodies many of the qualities that Horace Mann also exhibited. Like Mann, Gray left behind his known and safe Eastern world for a Western one in which he changed career direction to build a new and humanistic college. Like Antioch, the story of the early days of World College West and its founder are closely entwined. It is difficult to know one without the other.

Richard Gray was a precocious student who graduated from Bucknell at eighteen. He then spent 16 years as creative director for the N.W. Ayer advertising agency in Philadelphia when the death of his father made him reevaluate his life. He moved to California and from 1958 to 1961 was at the San Francisco Theological Seminary in San Anselmo, California for his M. Div. degree. After that instead of returning to business, he went into the campus ministry at Portland State, a community college for seven years. Then he went for his Ph.D. at Berkeley in Higher Education Administration where he conceptualized World College West.

The first years of the college were again similar to Antioch where Horace Mann had to personally support the college. Richard Gray sold his house to pay the first-year expenses. For the first eight years of its life World College West was in rented quarters at the San Francisco Theological Seminary. After that they moved into refurbished pre-World War II barracks at Fort Cronkhite on the Marin Headlands for three years. These years tested the strength of both the students and faculty as they carried on their academic rounds in drafty buildings with outside portable toilets on the windswept headlands overlooking the Pacific Ocean and San Francisco Bay.

In 1981 the college moved to a 194-acre campus on a hilltop in northern Marin which is reached by a twisting road lined with large oaks covered with lichens. The college was 28 miles from the Golden Gate bridge and enjoyed a year round Mediterranean-like climate.

Richard Gray voiced many of the ideas which lead to the development of World College West and the other utopian colleges when he stated:

> American higher education has been fed by three streams of tradition. One was the Ox-Bridge tutorial model, the liberal arts model. Second was the German research model. Third was the American utility model of agricultural and mining schools used to settle the frontier. All of this developed between 1860 and 1910; since then the American university has been struggling to determine what it really is. It has tried to be all things to all people and the undergraduates are usually the ones who get the short end of the stick, both in terms of learning through participation and in terms of student-faculty contact.[4]

Dr. Gray understood the historical background of American education when he made this statement in 1981, eight years after the founding of World College West and when they were moving onto their new campus. The traditional American models of either the German research institute, Ox-bridge tutorial, or utility model all had their examples in American education, and many were not working in a way to help the student. Gray further explained this problem when he said, "The German research model has sort of taken over; everything is geared to that. A graduate professor will work with five or six graduate students while a teaching assistant lectures to the undergraduates."[5] This is one of the reoccurring differences between the utopian colleges and the traditional system.

If World College West is not based on the German research model, then what model is it based upon? Dr. Gray explains:

> Basically there were three kinds of models. There is the transmission model, where the curriculum is passed along to the students. Second is the student-centered model, where students in the Sixties kind of did what they wanted to be doing. The third model was the collegial model, where you address a problem together. That's what we tried to draw on.[6]

The collegial model was used effectively at World College West and at the other utopian colleges. A respect and an exchange between students, faculty, trustees, and administrators existed on a daily basis. When Gray was the president of World College West, he was an example of this when he, as did other faculty members and administrators, helped to serve food to the students in the dining hall. The students worked on campus in clerical, landscaping, food preparation, and other jobs.

What kind of student went to this college? In 1981 Gray said: "I'd say thoughtful, humanizing change agents. . . . We're looking for reasonable adventurous people who have their act together enough to really stay with something."[7] The adventure of living in a foreign country as well as in a small college community was available to World College West students.

World College West followed many of the utopian tenets from its inception. Richard Gray, at the very beginning tried to call himself the "Spokesperson" rather than "President," while the other faculty-administrators were "Coordinators" rather than "Vice-Presidents." Since that time much of the governance system has been run through consensus which has been emphasized to a greater or lesser degree by different people, particularly by different presidents. A focus on undergraduate student development, which was the topic of Gray's Ph.D. dissertation, was present from the beginning.

Other philosophical beliefs which were incorporated into the fabric of the college were an emphasis on teaching, never on faculty publication. There were no faculty ranks or tenure. Letter grades were not used until 1991, and the emphasis was on the education of the whole person. A strong partnership always existed between the academic and experiential worlds, especially through the required internships and the foreign living and study experience. The whole community, students, faculty, and staff, were involved in the governance process.

The problems of survival seemed to be overcome in the first eight years of its existence, but the challenges of raising money and attracting quality, mature students continued with the college. After the initial survival and conceptualization phase of the college was accomplished, the question arose of what next? Many creative and highly talented people are drawn to a project or college in the early chaotic years, because they have an opportunity to create something new. What happens when the buildings are built, and the curriculum settles down?

In 1981 Gray answered:

> That's a big problem. We've talked about it quite a bit. What do you do for the second ten years—tear down the buildings and start again? I don't think that's it. But I think we'll work out something. I don't think I could stand another eight years like the last eight. [8]

Richard Gray had survived longer than Horace Mann did at approximately the same age under the similar conditions at Antioch.
When a charismatic leader creates, or helps to create, their ideal concept of an educational institution, the situation is similar to a utopian
system being put into practice, or the origins of a utopian community,
such as Oneida, being conceived and carried out by its strong leader.
The theoretical utopias were one thing on paper, but when they were
applied to actual situations in this world, many unknown outcomes
appeared, as with Brook Farm and Fourierism.

When a founder is replaced or retires, the community or college
must go through an intensive reevaluation. For instance, the charismatic personality of the founder allows the community to overlook
the fact that many community members do not agree on many issues.
They can find that it was the founder's personality , not their common
belief which held them together. When the founder is gone they often
are faced with sorting out their common beliefs and finding what is
the actual center of the community.

Michael Stone, the acting president of World College West during
the years of 1989–91, gave an interesting insight when he wrote:

> People who set out to create a community based on ideals counter to the
> prevailing culture may be unaware of how many of that culture's ideas they
> too hold. Or, they assume that because everyone in their community seeks an
> alternative to the mainstream culture, that means they all share the same
> alternative values, when in fact they may not. That's a World College West
> experience: "Because you and I are together at this alternative 'college,' you
> must share my disagreement with 'mainstream' education and culture on all
> points, and we must agree about what to replace it with."[9]

The next ten years from 1981 to 1991 that Richard Gray foresaw
as difficult were so difficult as to end the dream of World College West
which had taken form in an actual college on an actual mountain top
in California. In fact, Rollo May, the famous psychologist who served
on the board of trustees at World College West since its inception,
thought that "World College West is the college of the future. Its graduates are the planetary citizens who will be harbingers of a new way of
looking at the globe."[10] It may be the college of the future, since the
global village has become a reality.

In an article in the education section of the *New York Times*, World
College West was described as "one of a handful of small, progressive, experimental institutions that appeared on the American land-
scape in the early 70's."[11] In this article the writer identifies World

College West with the 60's and its "idealistic rhetoric." But is it rhetoric when a college survived for eighteen years carrying its utopian ideal into a working community on campus and a successful international program? The college achieved most of its original goals by 1990 and was a functioning reality with 120 students, 8 full-time faculty, and 25 adjunct faculty.

But the years between 1981 and 1992 were not easy ones. The difficult transition of the retirement of the founder in 1988 and his successor caused waves throughout the college community and almost brought the college to a standstill.

The *New York Times* article summaries the events:

> When Dr. Gray retired, the college faced perhaps its most arduous task: replacing him. His successor, Marcus Franda, a professor of economics and comparative politics, was concerned that students were not learning the practical skills they wanted and needed to compete in the workplace. Among Mr. Franda's priorities were raising money for a science and computer building and supporting the new business management major.
>
> Though his credentials were impeccable, his management style—perceived as autocratic—was anathema. He was not invited back.

The question of leadership style and values were the problem. A hierarchical "perceived as autocratic" man tried to apply the values on a then functioning community with the opposite values. A natural rejection of a foreign body in the community followed.

Michael Stone was the interim president who carried on the original values of the college. In 1990, Douglas Trout, who is a Presbyterian as are Richard Gray and Michael Stone, became the fourth president of the college. His background as a former college president and a believer in the original values of the college was supposed to heal the upheaval of the previous years. But in a college where the student faculty ratio is 12:1, the financial realities continue to be a part of the day-to-day life of the college.

Utopian colleges often have a setting and an atmosphere which inspires writers to describe them as such:

> If location is an indication of lofty academic goals, then World College West, the smallest four-year liberal arts college accredited by the Western Association of Schools and Colleges, is perfectly placed: perched on a hillside near Petaluma in rural northern Marin County, California, with a view that could easily inspire Utopian thinking.[13]

If "utopian thinking" is not allowed in American higher education and utopian colleges are not encouraged, then the academic system and the students will be the ones who will lose. These colleges need support from their graduates and their employers. They need financial aid from the government. They need the financial and moral support to continue their educational missions in their "utopian" settings.

World College West had trouble adjusting from its first generation to second generation. Its leadership tended to be patriarchal and not educated at progressive institutions which might explain the separation between many of its utopian concepts and the hierarchical systems which dominated on campus. The student body was more utopian and visionary than the faculty who was often traditional in their approach to education and to each other. The financial problems encouraged "crisis management" after the departure of Gray and in many cases allowed egos to dominate. This college was the least utopian of the five colleges in its administrative, clerical, and faculty structure which was traditional, but was the most visionary in global outlook. World College West was a noble and worthwhile experiment in higher education and its international concepts have been adopted by other institutions.

Notes

1   *World College West, 1990–91 Catalog,* p. 1.

2   Ibid, p. 1.

3   McNamara, Steve. "The Possible Dream." *Pacific Sun.* Oct. 9–15, 1981. p. 5.

4   Ibid, p. 5.

5   Ibid, p. 5.

6   Ibid, p. 5.

7   Ibid, p. 27.

8   Ibid, p. 8.

9   Stone, Michael. Notes. March 10, 1991.

10   Garfinkel, Perry. "Way Out West." *The New York Times.* Jan. 7, 1990.

11   Ibid.

12   Ibid.

13   Ibid.

Bibliography

1. Garfinkel, Perry. "Way Out West." *The New York Times*. Jan. 7, 1990.

2. McNamara, Steve. "The Possible Dream." *Pacific Sun*. Oct. 9–15, 1981.

3. Stone, Michael. Notes. March 10, 1991.

4. *World College West, 1990–91 Catalog.*

Chapter 11

Conclusion

After investigating the current status of American higher education, and in particular, the five identified colleges, these utopian colleges were found to have characteristics in common which were different than traditional American colleges. But trying to identify all five as "utopian colleges" provided a more difficult task than originally expected. Although most people would name these colleges and ones similar to them when asked to identify a "utopian college," the problem of a definition of "utopian" proved more slippery than when first addressed. The general public seemed to be substituting the word "utopian," for "progressive, experimental, or alternative" when describing these colleges.

When the top administrators or writers about these five colleges talk about their institutions, they usually trace their college's philosophical roots to former traditions or philosophers. For instance, Robert Conley traces the roots of Union to Oxford and Cambridge, the German research universities, and the American research universities of the fifties. Roy P. Fairchild traces the Union to Jean Jaques Rousseau, Friedrick Froebel, John Dewey, and the phenomenologists. Tim Pitkin went to William Heard Kilpatrick, John Dewey, and Bishop Grundtuig's Scandinavian folk schools for the inspiration of his years at Goddard. Harold Taylor followed the teachings of William James, Alfred North Whitehead, and John Dewey, as cited in *On Education and Freedom*, but writes in 1991 that "There was no orthodoxy or programmatic education cited, nor was there any suggestion that either I or the college would follow a pattern set by John Dewey, William Heard Kilpatrick or any other figure of importance in the progressive era."[1]

Although the presidents and writers of these colleges cited their philosophic and educational roots, they did not explain what it was in these traditions that fit their view of their institutions. What was the connection of Froebel and the phenomenoligists to The Union Institute as Roy Fairchild viewed it? He never explains. Harold Taylor cites Dewey and others throughout his speeches and books, but denies that he or Sarah Lawrence ever followed a pattern set by Dewey, Kilpatrick, or others in the progressive movement. The leaders of the utopian colleges were individualistic and "did their own thing" while citing their philosophic forefathers to substantiate their views, actions, and philosophies. Unfortunately, just the famous names identify the schools of thought and philosophies. A shorthand exists which needs to be filled out through further research, interviews, and questions. Within the limitations of this study, some of these philosophies and movements were briefly examined, but they often were not much better than extended annotated bibliographies which are a little more descriptive than the shorthand use of the names.

But in returning to the word, "utopia," which has a long, separate and valid history of its own, several different alternatives were open to the writer for its interpretation. One was to stake out ownership of the word and reject its history. Although that route was tempting, it could have proved dangerous. Another way would be to show that everything called "utopian" shares some characteristic goals and that some practices keep those utopians from achieving those goals. Again this was a tempting premise, but when applied it consisted of trying to stuff "square pegs into round holes." Many goals and practices did not fit. The third way was to realize that "utopian" means different things to different people. While my definition honors the history of utopian thinking and communities, the looser definition used expands to describe characteristics which all five colleges held in common.

These five institutions of learning represent both an "ideal" and a "good place." They all have struggled with the major educational problems of their time and have usually arrived at forward-thinking solutions. They went through cycles with good years and bad years. Some faced severe financial crises which threatened to close them, and in the case of World College West did just that. Some faced vicious attacks, such as Sarah Lawrence in the McCarthy era. They were not always perfect and often confronted ethical dilemmas, as did all of American higher education during trying times.

All of these colleges are usually utopian in concept and in the statements of their leaders and spokespeople, but all parts of the whole are not always utopian in reality. Ego, control, and selfishness arise in

both administrators and faculty. Students exploit others in their private lives. Boards of trustees become distanced from the problems of
students. Business decisions rather than ethical choices sometimes
eliminate worthwhile programs and reward self-serving ones. But in
their various and often parallel histories, these colleges were always
looked upon by the mainstream American culture as different from
other small colleges such as Mills, Pomona, Wittenberg, and Williams.
These colleges always contained the promise of intellectual and personal freedom. They were non-structured and encouraged free thinkers. They always caused a little unease in their surrounding communities. They were different; they dared to be utopian in a variety of
different ways. They were called "Communist," "hippie," "bohemian,"
"way-out," and "artsy," but they were never called "conservative," "bor-
ing," "stagnant," or "conventional." They all dared to test out their
utopian ideas in a variety of different ways leading to a variety of different results, some successful, some less so.

   The struggles of any utopian community of translating an ideal into
a working community takes the problem from theory or philosophy to
group dynamics and the vagaries of the "human condition." My conclusion is that there can be no "heaven on earth," but that utopian
plans and hopes are necessary with their attempts to try to achieve
better places rather than supporting the negative forces which encourage violence, racism, environmental destruction, and sexism. Although the world is difficult, the efforts to create better educational
places is laudatory and worth investigating.

   The similarities of these so-called utopian colleges are interesting
in light of the American culture. They do not have football teams which
is probably more of a result of their size than the ideological stance
which Hutchins encourages, while their size is a contributing factor to
their unique community atmosphere. When they grow too large, they
have difficulties in management and maintaining their ideals. But what
is "too large" is debatable. Hutchins uses the number of 250 students.
There is a loose universal number of 200 that anthropologists indicate
for effective lineage organization, and beyond this number groups
usually begin new lineages. When Goddard grew larger than that number, their community form of government ran into difficulties. Would
clusters of 250 oppose other clusters and evolve into a traditional
university? Sarah Lawrence has grown to over 1,000 students, but it
seems to maintain its original ethos and atmosphere. Antioch and
Goddard lost control when they had too many outposts. But what is

the number when this happens? Size is important, but it is not the only answer. The Union Institute instills its values in a mainly non-residential model of over 1000 learners.

These colleges are often faculty-run colleges with a student-centered education, or as Richard Gray of World College West described it as a "collegial model." Tenure does not stratify the faculty. Faculty clubs do not exist. Faculty do their own teaching and have the familiarity of Oxford dons with their students. The German research model which had taken over most American higher education is not found in these utopian colleges. Professors do research, create, and write, but not within the reward system of the research universities. No teaching assistants are used to distance the faculty from the students, and large lecture courses are rare. The criticism of large classes "lectured at" by uncaring professors which is a recurring issue in higher education today has been addressed at the utopian colleges where the give and take is in seminar-style classes encouraging individualized learning.

In these five colleges, the three non's: non-sexist, non-racist, and non-sectarian, were part of these colleges' original philosophy and are true today. Antioch has carried on these values for over one hundred and fifty years, which predated "progressive education" and the educational experiments of the sixties. This type of utopian higher education has run parallel to the traditional research universities, state-supported schools, traditional liberal arts colleges, community colleges, and the utility colleges of agricultural and mining schools used to settle the frontier. They are not just "hippie schools" created in the sixties, as some members of the press and the dominant culture try to categorize them.

The study of utopias and of utopian experiments was disheartening in a way that was not anticipated at the beginning of this project: They were mainly hierarchical and projections of male fantasies. When the colleges were studied, many of the same problems arose. Some of the colleges are moving to a hierarchical, top-down structure. Most of the colleges were created, ruled, and interpreted by their white male leaders. A female or minority voice was rare in the published works about these colleges. Only Sarah Lawrence, because it was a women's college, had women leaders writing and representing the college. The male leaders presented their utopias as they saw them. The reality, or others interpretations, were often different. Some male leaders criticized the previous male leaders and felt that their achievements far surpassed their predecessors, but often their attacks showed the same ego problems of their forerunners. The women in present day leadership positions tend to carry out the status quo of their male counter-parts. The contemporary women leaders often seem to be post-feminists or have a more conservative and traditional educational background than their faculty. These top women administrators rarely saw their colleges as experimental.

But these utopian colleges often have a more feminist attitude towards knowledge, education, and teaching. In the book *Women's Ways of Knowing*, the authors sum up their view of "women's development as the aim of education" when they state:

> We have argued in this book that educators can help women develop their own authentic voices if they emphasize connection over separation, understanding and acceptance over assessment, and collaboration over debate; if they accord respect to and allow time for the knowledge that emerges from firsthand experience; if instead of imposing their own expectations and arbitrary requirements, they encourage students to evolve their own patterns of work based on the problems they are pursuing. These are the lessons we have learned in listening to women's voices.[2]

The utopian colleges have often used these educational attitudes to develop not only their women students, but all of their learners. They have stressed "connection, understanding and acceptance, and collaboration." They also "accord respect to and allow time for the knowledge that emerges from firsthand experience" and "encourage students to evolve their own patterns of work based on the problems they are pursuing." From the philosophy that Horace Mann instilled in Antioch's early days to The Union Institute's continuing experiments in education, the utopian colleges have attempted to use these educational concepts in opposition to those used in traditional education.

Elizabeth Minnich in her book, *Transforming Knowledge*, goes beyond the "how's" of *Women's Ways of Knowing* to examine the "why's" of knowledge and knowing. She presents her theme as follows:

> The problem we still have today in thinking about the rich diversity of humankind is expressed by the observation that, at the beginning of the dominant Western tradition, a particular group of privileged men took themselves to be the inclusive term or kind, the norm, and the ideal for all, a "mis-taking" that is locked into our thinking primarily in the form of faulty generalizations, circular reasoning, mystified concepts that result from the former errors, and the partial (in both senses of the term) knowledge that frames such concepts.[3]

Minnich looks at the root of the problem and adds: "And I will suggest that the very same basic errors that have worked to perpetuate the exclusion of women do the same for the men of some groups as well, albeit without erasing gender hierarchy within those groups."[4] Her thinking applies to some men as well as women just as do the conclusions of Mary Belenky et al. "The rich diversity of humankind" can benefit from these equal approaches to education and knowledge. From the days at Antioch in the mid-1850's when women and African Americans were not excluded from the college to World College West where students lived in Third World countries, the utopian colleges have searched for education beyond the Western tradition. They have been open to diversity before it became a catchword both in their student body, faculty, and curriculum.

When I reflected on the conservative attacks on the humanities and the individualized education contained at the five colleges, I wondered whether all minority voices which need to be heard should be included as part of the backlash against feminism. The backlash seems to be against the opening of the higher educational system to the whole range of neglected voices and ways of knowing: women, minorities, non-Western, and non-elitist. Most of the basic beliefs of these five colleges are similar to feminist beliefs and benefit these neglected groups.

At this point the second definition of "utopia" should again be examined in the context of an educational institution existing on earth. The definition of "a place, state, or condition of ideal perfection, especially in laws, government, and social conditions" applied to all five colleges and to my general concept of what a utopian college should be.

"A place of ideal perfection" brings forth the arcadian dreams and the previously cited descriptions by journalists and visitors to some of these utopian colleges, i.e., Antioch in Yellow Springs and World College West on its idyllic hilltop in Marin County. All of the five colleges, plus the previously mentioned experimental colleges, have settings which seem to be inspired from an illustrated book of fairy tales. Even the non-residential Union is now headquartered in a clock-towered Tudor building with Grimm's fairy tale overtones. Although a utopian college could be located in an urban setting, these are not. From the large Tudor mansions of Sarah Lawrence and Union to the small villages with the colleges as their focus surrounded by farmland and forests, as with Antioch and Goddard, to the "never-never land" hilltop approached by a winding road through the gnarled, lichen-hung trees of the former World College West, all of these colleges evoke a "utopian" place description.

But what is not visually first apparent about these places is the "utopian" lifestyle and mindset which they encourage. These are places where their inhabitants, whether they be students, professors, or administrators, have a protected space where they can safely live and create. Women can walk on the college grounds and not be attacked. A diversity of students inhabit these utopian places.

For a woman many of the large research institutions have areas that are off limits and are unsafe at night and sometimes the day. Many large universities now have patrols and student escorts for women to protect them from assault and rape. The libraries, faculty clubs, and some parts of the traditional campuses are not open to outside visitors while the libraries, all eating places, and administrative offices in the five utopian colleges were open and accessible to anyone who is either part of the campus or a visitor.

The question arises whether *all* small rural and suburban colleges are "safe places" while large, urban universities near crime areas are unsafe? This is a question that someone else must study and answer, but for this paper on utopian colleges my personal experience of walking on, eating at, and observing over fifty American campuses did produce a point of view. My observations were that the utopian colleges had a more relaxed atmosphere than most of the other institutions. Whether this attitude is created because of the lack of a competitive grading system, an absence of professional, money-making athletic programs, or other factors is unknown. What is obvious to the visitor is the non-segregated intermingling of students, faculty, and administrators who eat together in large communal dining rooms which usually feature vegetarian and other health-oriented food. Goddard, World College West, and Sarah Lawrence were especially communal in their eating situations, while Antioch was less so and the Union not at all, because of its mainly non-residential structure. The sense of community was strongest at World College West and Goddard and so was their communal gathering over meals.

Although all of these colleges are located at a "place," or home base, they encourage students in their programs to be part of the world. Even though these campuses are often arcadian in setting, they are no ivory towers where professors do their own research for publication and shun the students. These faculty are involved in the excitement of teaching in small classes and in individual conferences. This intense teaching model which usually occurs in a circle in a seminar-style classroom around a table produces lively discussions and interactions which spill out into public places where students and teachers are seen having lunch, meeting on the campus, and walking together. In the traditional universities where lecture style classrooms and a hierarchical system prevail, I observed students with other students, usually of their own ethnic background, while the faculty clubs, hidden meeting rooms, and offices isolated the full-time professors and top administrators.

In the utopian colleges the students learn and are safe in their own home base college, but use the world as a classroom. Antioch introduced the work-study program which has been adopted by other colleges. Only a portion of Antioch students are in residence in Yellow Springs while the others are living and working in the field. World College West was the first American college to require every student to study abroad with a total immersion in the culture of a non-Western country. Sarah Lawrence and Antioch have maintained foreign centers. The graduate programs of Union and Goddard have students studying independently throughout the world. The students at utopian colleges are being trained to live in the "global village." The utopian colleges educate students who carry the college's philosophical beliefs with them to work-study jobs in East L.A. or Third World immersion.

The second item in the description of "utopia" after "place" is a "state of ideal perfection." A state can be a "state, or form of government," or a "state of mind" which is what these colleges often are. The actual government of a utopian college is at its best when it works as a community and at its worst when it falls into the hierarchical and bureaucratic traps that ensnare much of traditional higher education. Both Goddard and Antioch suffered when they lost their sense of community. Sarah Lawrence and The Union Institute have learned to combine the utopian ideal with sound financial planning and management. Participation of faculty, trustees, and students working together can create an economic balance. A system of openness and community should be able to co-exist with financial stability.

As a "state of mind" these colleges have become utopian. Their graduates often acquire a far-off look when they talk about their years at Sarah Lawrence, Goddard, World College West, Antioch, or The Union Institute. Not having just the traditional university nostalgia of college football games, sorority and fraternity parties, and being a "big man on campus" or the "sweetheart of Sigma Chi" which many traditional American graduates remember, these graduates have memories of a place where their ideas were important. They remember a place where they were listened to by respected teachers, and where for a few years they developed their own paths of learning not dictated by job descriptions or parents. They remembered the freedom to be what they wanted to be and not be silenced or excluded. They were allowed to be the individuals who could act creatively in an environment different than at home or in the dominant American culture. Their "state of mind" often produced an intellectual and creative "altered state" where they thought and created in a way beyond, even their own expectations.

The first two definitions bring us to the last which encompasses the first two: "a condition of ideal perfection." What is this condition of ideal perfection which I observed in the five colleges? What do these "progressive" and "experimental" colleges have that traditional education has lost or never had?

Being a woman, I experienced a rare phenomenon as a student, visitor, or professor at these colleges when I was treated with as much dignity and equality as if I had been a white male. The small seminar style of teaching at Sarah Lawrence allowed equal participation and discussion among students. My graduate seminar at Columbia University was instead a platform for two rude and vocal male graduate students who dominated the discussions. When any woman attempted to speak, she was shouted down or ridiculed by these students as the young, frightened male teaching assistant observed. One might say that this was because it was the sixties. But this same phenomena occurred at Sonoma State University in 1990 in a critical thinking class. When the class was taken outdoors and formed a circle for open discussion, it split into two groups. The divided group watched as two young white male student/bucks verbally locked horns while the rest of the class became passive herd observers. The white, male professor encouraged the two aggressive young men who received A's for their performance.

At the utopian colleges *all* students are given as much freedom, power, and upward mobility as white men. This is a heady experience for members of oppressed groups, and this includes women, who have been silenced or ignored before. They know within the relatively safe boundaries of their college environment they can speak and be themselves. Because of this educational experience in a utopian setting, they become "empowered" to try to carry their voice and their experience into the outside culture.

My experience has not always been ideal or been "a condition of ideal perfection" at these colleges. A sexist undertone prevailed from one administration while I was at Goddard. A male professor at a Union seminar kept recognizing the male learners but not calling on the women participants. At Sarah Lawrence Joseph Campbell was paternalistic to his female students. It is interesting to note that Campbell was the only professor at Sarah Lawrence who lectured and pontificated *at* his students, as he did in his TV series. He performed in the standard forum of traditional education: A usually male professor lecturing *at* an audience or class of silent student observers.

What is unusual about these utopian colleges is not where they fail to live up to their lofty ideals, but that they succeed in so many ways and keep struggling to achieve their professed "conditions of ideal perfection" in an increasingly difficult world where the dominant culture is hypocritical, materialistic, and cynical. Any utopian college needs financial support and an enlightened student body, faculty, board of trustees, and administrators. All of these supporters are drawn from a hostile dominant culture, so that when these colleges and universities can still grow and survive, it is a miracle. These miracles and utopias must continue to exist, so that future generations of participants can experience a safe place where minds can develop with individualized education and in small, supportive learning groups where all are heard, not silenced. These students must have access to the learned and the top people in their field, not just to teaching assistants. Women and ethnic groups must be allowed as much freedom, power, and upward mobility as white men, at least in the few years of their educational process. The learners must be able to use their abilities and not be constantly competitive towards others. They need the safety to move about, speak, and live without being harassed. Utopian colleges are needed in America and the world today.

But a utopian vision has difficulties in translation into a workable form on earth either as a utopian community or college whether it has a feminist ideology, an improvement of all society as in Hutchin's University of Utopia, or other utopias from Plato to More to Bellamy. Both Bellamy and Hawthorn thought "a colony was not a test of the workability of the doctrines it supported."[5] What was reassuring and hopeful in the investigation of the five colleges was how many of their stated ideals and much of their "utopian thinking" was achieved in their working educational models. Some institutions are more financially secure than others, but they still espouse their particular dreams which differentiate them from traditional higher education. Critics of our higher education system today should look to the working models of a "utopian education" in our midst for some examples to help solve some of their educational problems.

Notes

1. Utopian Colleges, p. 126.

2. Belenky, Mary Field, Clinchy Blythe McVicker, Goldberger, Goldberger, Nancy Rule, Tarule, Jill Matluck. *Women's Ways of Knowing: The Development of Self, Voice, and Mind.* Basic Books, Inc. Publishers: New York, 1986. p. 229.

3. Minnich, Elizabeth Kamarch. *Transforming Knowledge.* Temple University Press: Philadelphia, 1990. p. 2.

4. Ibid, p. 3.

5. Utopian Colleges, p. 10.

Bibliography

1. Belenky, Mary Field, Clinchy Blythe McVicker, Goldberger, Nancy Rule, Tarule, Jill Matluck. *Women's Ways of Knowing: The Development of Self, Voice, and Mind*. Basic Books, Inc. Publishers: New York, 1986.

2. Minnich, Elizabeth Kamarch. *Transforming Knowledge*. Temple University Press: Philadelphia, 1990.

Index